# 300 DECORATING IDEAS under $100

# CONTENTS

# what can you do with $100?

When you're in the mood to do something wonderful to your home or yard, we hope this collection will inspire you to create. Each idea will cost less than $100, and many under $50. We've even provided instructions to help you assemble beautiful accents for every room in the house.

You may have many of the materials at hand. Some of the window treatments, for example, start with what you have, then customize with small amounts of fabric and trims and clever use of hardware. We've included easy slipcovers that will fit over chairs you already own. You'll also find numerous wall treatments that require little paint, so keep those leftovers from other projects—you already know those colors match the decor.

If you've done any construction or remodeling recently, save the small pieces of trim and molding. You'll be surprised at what you can do with so-called scraps! Put broken tile to good use on a backsplash or hearth. And be sure to look up to the ceiling, often a forgotten feature, for another decorating surface. Embellishing the area around a light fixture, for instance, gives you a built-in spotlight for your work.

So, now that you have this book in hand, you can get started right away. When you do, we think you'll move on to more than just the first project. Why? Because we've made sure that each one is easy and affordable, but most of all, simply beautiful!

Enjoy!

The Staff

# Better Homes and Gardens®
## Creative Collection™

**Director, Editorial Administration**
Michael L. Maine

**Editor-in-Chief**
Beverly Rivers

**Executive Editor** Karman Wittry Hotchkiss

| **Editorial Manager** | **Art Director** |
| Ann Blevins | Don Nickell |

**Copy Chief** Mary Heaton
**Administrative Assistant** Lori Eggers
**Contributing Graphic Designer** Lauren Luftman
**Contributing Copy Editors** David Walsh,
Wendy Wetherbee
**Contributing Proofreader** Joleen Ross

---

**Vice President, Publishing Director**
William R. Reed

---

**Group Publisher** Steve Levinson
**Senior Marketing Manager** Suzy Johnson

---

CORPORATION

**Chairman and CEO**
William T. Kerr

---

**In Memoriam**
E. T. Meredith III (1933–2003)

---

**Publishing Group President**
Stephen M. Lacy
**Magazine Group President**
Jack Griffin

# wall displays

Try these easy innovations to elevate wall elements into artistic eye-catchers.

# out on a rung

1

In flea market decorating, utilitarian objects gain importance. A weathered ladder, hung horizontally from decorative brackets, steps out in style as a quilt rack. Give the ladder a fresh coat of paint, or let it show its rustic side. **another idea:** Prop a ladder vertically against a bathroom wall to create a towel rack.

# 2
# handy
# hangers

When out scavenging, look for decorative items that can bring function to your home. This piece of garden fence takes up little space in an entry and is just the right size for organizing children's jackets.

# iron works

Rescued from a garage sale for just $10, a metal screen-door protector, *left*, becomes a work of art by displaying old photos. A coat of matte-finish black spray paint hides imperfections and adds to the graphic appeal. **another idea:** Old metal garden gates and fretwork make equally stunning art pieces.

# a rose is a rose

As pretty as a dozen long-stem roses, a collection of vintage botanical prints leaves its own fresh scent in the monochromatic room at *right*. Grouped en masse, the 19th-century heirloom rose illustrations emphasize the room's lofty scale. To ensure that the focus stays on the flowers, the prints were mounted without mats in simple discount-store frames painted white. Touches of patterned fabrics unify the delicate floral scheme, providing another blush of color. Look for budget-pleasing botanical prints in old books, calendars, and magazines.

# on display

Put a favorite collection on view with an innovative showcase fashioned from a peeling multipane window frame, a piece of molding, and drawer knobs. Use wood glue to attach the molding to the top of the window frame; let dry. (If desired, skip this step and use the window frame without a topper.) Drill holes into the frame, centering above each pane in the window. Screw a knob or hook, available at home improvement stores, into each hole. Hang vintage handbags on the knobs or hooks. **another idea:** Collections of hats, small baskets, teacups, dried flowers, or ornaments also suspend nicely from the knobs.

# 6

## frame of reference

Weathered textures team with time-softened colors that convey a sense of gentle aging in the cottage-style living room at *left*. On the mantel, the graphic arrangement of frames (minus their pictures), wooden spindles, an iron bracket, and a wire trivet offers a composition lesson. The overlapping frames carve out negative spaces of different sizes, while contrasting shapes rest on the frames' edges. Candlesticks enclose the primitive arrangement.

## order in the house

Thoughtful framing and placement eliminate chaos when assembling a collage of antique photos. Collect frames from the same general era, painting all of them white for a unified look. How-to instructions begin on page 226.

# 7

# 8
## words of wisdom

Make a subtle, tasteful statement.
Framing favorite quotations with wide
white mats and narrow black frames
draws attention to the words while
keeping them from shouting their
messages across the room.
How-to instructions begin on page 226.

Don't regret growing older.
It is a privilege denied by many.
*Anonymous*

Make it a rule never to regret and never to look back.
*Marjorie Kinnan Rawlings*

No great artist ever sees things as they really are.
If he did, he would cease to be an artist.
*Oscar Wilde*

# 9
## knock, knock

Old door hardware is elaborate and artful—it
deserves a place of honor in an antiques
collector's home. When framed against
decorative papers, the pieces showcase
intricate workmanship.
How-to instructions begin on page 226.

# take a tint

Tinting photographs makes a display look aged while drawing out the hues of the room. To further coordinate the look, mat the pictures on fabrics that complement the room and place them in identical frames.

How-to instructions begin on page 226.

## set sail **11**

For a nautical theme, you'll find a boatload of possibilities. A ship's ladder from an old freighter has steps the right width to display a collection of boats gathered from flea markets. **another idea:** Oars, a life preserver, roping, or a captain's hat also offer seafaring style.

## 12
## in-depth analysis

Make your artwork three-dimensional by mounting family memorabilia directly to the wall—then surround them with a frame. If you don't have enough personal items to fill the frames, augment the collection with finds from flea markets and antiques stores.

How-to instructions begin on page 226.

## 13
## shadow play

Who says a still life has to be still? A small ledge in a shadow-box-style frame holds a floral arrangement that even van Gogh couldn't duplicate. When fresh flowers are too fleeting, substitute silk flowers or a small sculpture.

How-to instructions begin on page 226.

# a chair
# affair

Find yourself sitting pretty

with slipcover and paint projects that

transform worn furniture

into works of art.

# 14
## a serene update

More affordable than upholstering, slipcovers still offer outstanding options. To update a wood-frame chair, spray-paint the frame and let dry; then brush with steel wool to "wear" the paint in places. Apply a few coats of polyurethane to help the finish endure. For the slipcover, use a slightly darker underlining fabric to highlight the pattern in a sheer top layer. To make the ribbon trim, pin 2½- to 3-inch loops of ribbon to bias tape, top them with another piece of bias tape, and machine-stitch. Sew the trim to the bottom of the fabric as you would any other fringe.

# 15
## boudoir beauty

Dress a bedroom chair in a bustling romantic skirt. For this chair, velvet adorns the seat and back, and prepleated ecru silk outfits the full skirt. Tiny fabric roses, available from fabrics stores, are spaced at 6-inch intervals around the skirt. To make the matching cabbage rose pillow, fold an 8-inch-wide strip of fabric lengthwise, threading lightweight wire between the layers. Spiral the fabric, shaping it into a large rose, and sew it atop a 12-inch round pillow form covered in matching silk.

# 16
## cheer for a tie

Who would know an ordinary folding chair hides beneath this cover? Two flat pieces of fabric sewn together are held to the chair with ribbon ties.

How-to instructions begin on page 226.

# 17 classy cover

For an elegant look, slipcover a solid-wood chair. This tailored topper resembles a Swedish pinafore with dual layers of fabric, crocheted lace near the top, piping at the seams, and a gracefully arched hem edged with ribbon. To make this slipcover, choose medium-weight taupe-and-cream gingham and ivory linen. For a smooth ribbon border, don't arch the hem too deeply. A few small gathers help the ribbon lie flat. If your machine doesn't do monograms, have one made on a separate piece of fabric. Center the monogram from side to side and slightly higher than the center from top to bottom. To avoid wrinkles and shifting, use hook-and-loop fastening tape to close the cover at the back.

## sew what?

A flirty little skirt adds softness and femininity to a curvy chair. Best of all, this little slip is made with no sewing. How-to instructions begin on page 226.

## a star in stripes

Change style with a change of dress. Awning stripes echo the casual straight lines of this chair. A fancy fabric, such as toile, would make a formal statement. How-to instructions begin on page 226.

18

19

# 20
## rounding things out

A scallop-edge pinstripe cover looks like a pretty little pinafore. The curves at the bottom are a good match for the shapely rounded top.

How-to instructions begin on page 226.

# 21
## display a soft side

When you don't want to hide the graceful architecture of a chair but want to soften the lines a bit, enhance the chair with a slipcover made of filmy fabric.

How-to instructions begin on page 226.

# 22
## old softies

Create a dressing chair that's a pleasure to sit on. Terry cloth is comfortable, absorbent, and easy to care for. When the slipcover needs cleaning, throw it in the washing machine with your bathrobe.

# 23
## the great cover-up

Bistro chairs, excelling in style and convenience, often lack in comfort. Soften both the look and feel of wood or metal chairs with brightly patterned padded covers.
How-to instructions begin on page 226.

# 24
## letter perfect

Plain fabric accented with an appliqued monogram and piping creates a decidedly formal look for this chair. Use one letter for all the chairs, or give each one an initial of its own.
How-to instructions begin on page 226.

# in a new
# light

These simple, illuminating ideas
transform plain fixtures into shining stars.

# 25
## crystal clear

With glistening crystals and a delicate design, this lacy lamp shade seems far from the bargain it is. The "lace" is actually art paper, and the crystals were stripped from an old chandelier. Though we put this showstopper atop vintage glass, the shade would be just as pretty on a painted wood or sleek silver base, available at discount stores. Look for chandelier crystals at antiques stores, at lighting stores, or in the lighting section of home centers.

How-to instructions begin on page 226.

# 26
## uplifting effect

Tiny chandelier shades sport different patterns for drama. Bold colors and geometric designs unite for a coordinated lighting statement. How-to instructions begin on page 226.

## 27

# sticky situation

This technique has guaranteed good results.
A paper shade painted in hues of yellow is embellished
with floral stickers. If the garden motif doesn't suit your
decor, check stationery stores for other stickers.

## 28

# added texture

Making this lamp at *near left* is almost as much fun as a day at
the beach. Paint the plain plaster base, then cover the neck with
tiny shells. Add starfish to the shade to carry out the theme.

Decorative studs and cording add texture to a simple shade at
*far left*. The lamp base and shade can be painted to add even
more interest.

How-to instructions begin on page 226.

# 29
## fabric fancy

A shade fashioned from sheer and green-quilted fabrics creates a cozy glow. To achieve this look, remove the paper shade from the wire base. Sew sheer fabric into a tube the circumference of the wire base. Hem the bottom, and accent with green fabric. Fold the top over the wire base; secure with fabric glue.

# lasting impressions

With pastel hues that seem plucked from a Monet painting, a plain white fabric lamp shade becomes the canvas for a work of art. The Impressionistic design for the cabbage rose lamp shade was painted with acrylic crafts paints thinned with water. Brushed onto the shade as random spirals, the diluted paint bleeds through the shade's fibers to create the watercolor effect. Because every fabric shade has its own artistic personality, the watercolor effect is unpredictable but usually pleasing.

How-to instructions begin on page 226.

# refreshing a classic

For a makeover in minutes, cover a shade with fabric and add a few trims. To complement the vintage base of this lamp, we chose dotted Swiss fabric for the shade and ball fringe for edge trim. Many fabrics stores sell small, ready-to-cover shades for less than $10. Peel off the paper liner to reveal the adhesive; then use the paper you removed as a pattern to cut the fabric. To cover a nonadhesive shade, lay the shade on its side atop the fabric. Roll the shade over the fabric, using a pencil to trace along the top and bottom. Cut the fabric slightly larger than the pencil marks. Test the fabric's fit on the shade, trimming as needed. Use spray adhesive to adhere the fabric to the shade. Glue fringe to the top and bottom to cover the raw edges.

# 32 | wallpaper wise

Before you toss wallpaper scraps or borders, consider gluing them onto lamp shades to complement your room's decor.

START TO FINISH

STEP 1. Start with a purchased shade.

STEP 2. Cut a strip of wallpaper or border twice the circumference of the shade bottom; for height, cut it ½ inch longer than the shade.

STEP 3. Use a pencil to mark pleats every ½ inch on wallpaper backing (using the length of the wallpaper).

STEP 4. Fold the paper accordion style, using the pencil marks and a straightedge as guides to keep the pleats straight.

STEP 5. Glue the cover to the shade along the top and bottom edges, overlapping the last pleat. To finish, glue decorative ribbon around the top and bottom of the shade.

# 33
## trendy tiers

Go ultramod with this futuristic lamp, which is surprisingly easy to make.

START TO FINISH

STEP 1. Adhere white round stickers randomly to the outside of three 7-inch linen lamp shades.

STEP 2. Lay a shade on a large piece of sheer art paper. Rolling the shade as you go, trace its entire top and bottom: You should end up with a U shape.

STEP 3. Cut out the art paper, position it on the shade to make sure it fits, and attach with spray adhesive. Repeat with the remaining shades.

STEP 4. Using crafts glue, join the three shades; let dry.

STEP 5. Remove the harp from the top and bottom shades. Position the shade on the lamp using the middle harp.

# timely statement

Here's a timely look. A paper shade, painted to match the room, is covered with clock faces from a clip-art book. You can find almost any theme in clip art, but be sure to keep the shapes simple.

How-to instructions begin on page 226.

# a rosy outlook 35

Even if you don't have a green thumb, you can grow a tiny rose garden. All it takes is some light (in the form of the lamp and shade) and a few dozen silk roses. The vase-shape lamp base accentuates the floral theme.

# natural shade

Leaves scattered over a paper shade bring the look of nature indoors. Cut the leaf shape from painter's tape and apply it to the shade. Then paint the shade to match the room. Remove the tape carefully to reveal white leaves.

How-to instructions begin on page 226.

# 37
## classy cutout

Accent a bedside table with a handcrafted lamp shade and mosaic lamp base. Make your own cutout shade with a kit from a crafts store or use lamp-shade paper. Stencil a design on the paper; cut out with a crafts knife. Add a parchment-paper liner designed for lamps or create your own following the steps above and using parchment paper. Apply the shade to the wire lamp frame as directed; glue and clamp until dry. Use a 60-watt or lower bulb only.

# 38
## candle makers

Multipatterned paper napkins cover candle lamps, matching them to a distinct china pattern. Look for napkins that match or coordinate with your china for a unifying effect.

How-to instructions begin on page 226.

## illuminating photos 39

Bring your favorite family photos out of storage for everyday enjoyment. Decorate a shade with old snapshots for an antique look with special meaning.

# perfect pair

**40**

We looked beyond a lacquer of harvest gold to give this $10 pair of garage-sale lamps a makeover. A coat of butter-yellow glossy paint with white accents transforms the bases. New scallop-pattern shades repeat the detail of the bases. Beaded trim glued around the shades' bottom edges offers the final flourish. The lesson? When you find two-of-a-kind lamps on the cheap, buy them. Having a pair offers design flexibility and a more cohesive look.

# window
## wizardry

Greet the light of a new day with
out-of-the-ordinary
window treatments that boast luxurious
fabrics and sleek shades.

  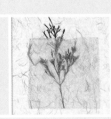 

## 11

## have a ball

Rows of ball fringe soften this cornice and draw your eye to the window.
Pack the balls tightly and glue on with fabric paste to form a chenille-like
surface. Trim draperies with the fringe as well for a coordinated look.

## go to great lengths

If your windows are too tall for standard draperies, extend their looks. A floral band sewn to the bottom edge makes these tall windows look shorter—and more inviting.

# 43
## side treatment

A few quick embellishments add pizzazz to a plain piqué panel. Ribbon ties, daisy trim, a stylish rod, and draping the curtain to one side update this window in minutes. How-to instructions begin on page 226.

# 44 sheer magic

Tall transom windows don't require custom window treatments. Sew sheer fabric to standard sizes and trim with cording and ties. This will add length to the window treatment and allow light into the room. How-to instructions begin on page 226.

# 45 casual or formal

Tailor plain muslin panels with ribbon trim and matching buttons to fit the style of your room. Use grosgrain ribbon and flat-finish buttons for a casual look or satin ribbon and shiny buttons for a more formal effect. How-to instructions begin on page 226.

# 46 dyed design

Spice up plain fabrics with something from the fridge—yellow mustard and vinegar—for an irresistibly delicious-looking window. How-to instructions begin on page 226.

47

## 48
## bygone times

Two '60s favorites—ball fringe and grommets—
have resurfaced in the fashion and decorating
worlds. Here, they add playful bounce to ordinary
tinted sheers.

How-to instructions begin on page 226.

## dish-towel delight

For a casual kitchen or dining room window
treatment, drape dish towels through napkin rings
strung on a tension rod. We found simple white-
striped towels at a discount store for $1.99 and
teamed them with hammered metal napkin rings.
Hang the rings on the tension rod, then position
the rod in the middle of the window. Loop a dish
towel through each ring, adjusting the towels so
the tips droop almost to the windowsill. **another
idea:** Take the in-a-jiff treatment up high to create
a valance. Vary towel colors or patterns for a
multicolor treatment.

## turning the table

Almost any attractive piece of fabric can answer the call to window stardom. The light,
airy window treatment *opposite* is actually a lace tablecloth. You may even have a
likely prospect in your linen closet. After measuring the window, choose material that's
wider than your window and at least the length from the curtain rod to the floor. If the
tablecloth is longer, fold over the top to create a valance as shown. To hang, simply
attach the cloth to a rod using clip-on drapery rings (see *inset photo*). Gather the
curtain toward the center at windowsill height and tie with a ribbon. **another idea:**
Choose two matching tablecloths and pull open from the center, tying each cloth
to the side.

# 50

## stamp of approval

Perfectly fine becomes
perfectly fantastic when stamped
with a subtle floral design.
Stamps and ink pads made
especially for fabrics are available
at stamping supply stores.
How-to instructions begin on
page 226.

51

## ribbon revival

You don't have to settle for plain white curtain panels when a trip to a
fabrics or crafts store yields so many decorating possibilities. We
enhanced these ready-made panels at *left* with lengths of ribbon sewn
vertically. Be sure to use washable ribbon, and measure your curtain
carefully to determine the total yardage needed. Then edgestitch the
ribbon in place and tie the ends around a curtain rod to hang.

## link effect 52

Opaque and sheer fabrics fastened with ribbons laced through grommets team up in this window treatment. A diamond-patterned valance makes a visually compelling topper; and a striped sheer its wispy foil. The top layer of sheer fabric is cinched in the center with 1-inch-wide ribbon.

# 53
## tassel toppers

Top a plain velvet drapery panel with a tassel-tipped pennant valance. Satin-covered buttons hide the stitches that tack the two treatments together.

How-to instructions begin on page 226.

# 54
## coordination counts

Two pairs of unlined draperies in coordinating fabrics join forces in a richly patterned window treatment that shows its stuff when buttoned back.

How-to instructions begin on page 226.

# café casual

Bring the look and warm feeling
of a neighborhood café into any room.

## paper pockets

55

Handmade paper is a soft and sturdy material
for covering windows. The paper gently
diffuses light, and pocketed flowers create
a unique motif.

How-to instructions begin on page 226.

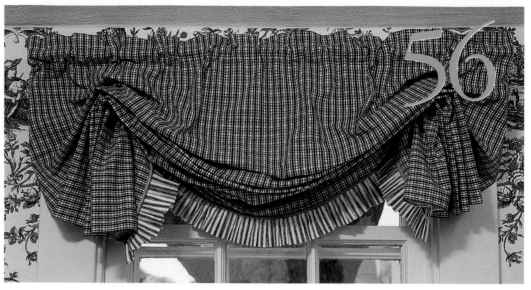

56

## same but different

Contrasting prints in the same colors, piped in a third color, give lots of interest to a simple swag. Ring tape used on Roman shades shapes the swag, yet makes laundering and ironing easy.

How-to instructions begin on page 226.

57

## paper penny-pinchers

In a pinch? Don't throw in the towel. Just toss some decorative art paper over a towel bar, pinch a few pleats, add some ribbon, and call it a curtain. We chose lacy art paper for these cute pinch-pleat curtains at *left*. Select decorative paper (available at art supply and crafts stores) that is soft, sturdy, and translucent.

How-to instructions begin on page 226.

58

## in the swing

Here's an open-and-shut case: The swing-arm-rod panels at *right* are both stylish and functional. With decorative paper mounted on movable rods, the window treatment offers privacy or a view of the outdoors. Install the top pair of rods right side up, and the bottom pair upside down. Raffia laced through punched holes holds the paper panels to the rods.

How-to instructions begin on page 226.

## 59 all buttoned up

Transform cloth napkins into pretty curtains. You'll need two to four napkins per panel, depending on the size of your window. Fold under 3 inches of the top napkin to create a rod pocket. Sew on five evenly spaced buttons, stitching through both layers of fabric to secure. Pin a second napkin to the bottom of the first, overlapping it 3 inches. Join the two napkins with five more buttons. Repeat the process for each panel until you reach the desired length.

## bead works

60

A few yards of acrylic beaded trim adds little cost but lots of sparkle to an elegant white-on-white valance. Sew the trim to the edge of the purchased valance, or make your own.
How-to instructions begin on page 226.

## case study

Take advantage of the decorative hems and baglike construction of pillowcases to turn them into window treatments. The pillowcase curtains at *left* completely cover the small window, but they also could be hung as café curtains. A pair of white cutwork pillowcases sheath vibrant floral fabrics with a ruffled hem for a soft look. Pretty ribbons hold the curtains to the rod.
How-to instructions begin on page 226.

# glass windows

Change the ordinary into see-worthy sensations with a few easy moves.

## 62
### no peeking

Dressing windows on a front door or sidelight can be tricky. Make it simple with an easy-on, easy-off film that's like wallpaper for windows and mimics the look of etched glass. This treatment provides privacy yet still lets sunlight in. The film also is a nifty solution on bathroom windows or other places where privacy matters. Look for the film, such as removable and reusable Wallpaper for Windows, at home centers. Simply cut the film to size, peel off its backing paper, and position it on a water-misted window. Window dressings don't get much easier than this!

How-to instructions begin on page 226.

## 63
### mirror, mirror

The look of stained or leaded glass is within easy reach—and it's not just for windows. We used self-adhesive leading strips, simulated liquid lead, and glass paint to create this stained-glass-look mirror. The easy-to-use products that simulate the look of stained or leaded glass are readily available at crafts stores. To start, have a glass supplier cut a piece of plain mirror with a smooth, ground edge, but you can use a ready-made mirror. (A mirror with a beveled edge is hard to work with, so choose another style.) Mounted to foam-core board, the stained-glass mirror is light enough to be held with wire gallery clips, available at art and framing stores.

How-to instructions begin on page 226.

# can-do curtain

This lacy window design is so dainty and intricate, no one will ever guess it came from a can. A soiled lace tablecloth and a can of enamel spray paint were all it took to create the gauzy eye-stopper on the lower pane. Adhere an old tablecloth or a piece of inexpensive by-the-yard lace to the glass, then lightly apply a coat of white spray paint to the window. Remove the lace to reveal the design. With the money you save by painting the "curtain," you'll be able to splurge on a delicate lace valance. How-to instructions begin on page 226.

64

65

# privacy pattern

Etching bathroom glass is an easy way to let in light while preserving privacy.

**START TO FINISH**

STEP 1. Clean the glass thoroughly and mask off molding with low-tack painter's tape.

STEP 2. Place small stickers on the windowpanes in a pattern that complements your room's decor.

STEP 3. When applying etching cream, protect your hands with rubber gloves and make sure the room is well ventilated.

STEP 4. Using a foam brush to minimize streaking, apply a thick layer of etching cream over the windowpanes, brushing horizontally, then vertically. After about 5 minutes, the glass will be permanently etched, except where covered by stickers.

STEP 5. Remove the etching cream with clean rags and water; peel off the stickers and painter's tape. Nail-polish remover will clean away any residue left by the stickers.

# shades&blinds

Combining beauty with practicality,
what goes up—and down—becomes an
eye-pleasing style setter.

## roll with it

**66**

Add a warm, casual touch to your child's room with a fleece roller shade. Stitch decorative edging to form the seams, and hang from a curtain rod. To open the shade, roll the fleece to the desired height, and button it into place on colorful twill tape.

# 67

# the ties that bind

Give matchstick blinds designer style with decorative fabric ties. For each tie, cut a fabric strip twice the length of the window, and about 7 inches wide. With right sides facing, fold each strip in half lengthwise. Using a ½-inch seam allowance and leaving an opening for turning, sew across the bottom of the strip, up the long edge, and across the opposite end. Turn the tie right side out and hand-sew the opening closed; press. Loop each tie over the blinds and tie into a bow. **another idea:** For a no-sew tie, press each fabric strip under ½ inch on all edges; then press lengthwise with wrong sides together, sandwiching fusible tape between edges to adhere. Or use ribbon instead of fabric ties.

# 68
## pretty patchwork

A colorful patchwork shade—
made from paper-backed silk
used to bind books—shimmers
on these standard windows.
Squares are arranged randomly
for unexpected punches of color.
For a 36x48-inch shade, cut
fabrics in 6-inch squares using a
quilter's grid and rotary cutter for
straight edges. Iron the squares
onto a standard roller shade so
the edges touch. If the white
background shows between
the squares, hide it with strips of
ribbon attached with fusible tape.

# 69
## map it out

A map-motif valance, cut to the shapes of the continents,
pairs with an embellished standard pull-down shade for a
classic maritime look. The valance hangs on rings from
a decorative brass rod finished with painted sphere finials
and roping.

# 70
## towel time

Dress your kitchen windows in style with shades made from tea towels. Window widths and towel sizes vary, so mix and match them for a pretty patchwork pattern.
How-to instructions begin on page 226.

# 71
## international view

For worldly style in a home office or for inspiration in a child's room, create a stimulating map window shade. This window treatment starts with an inexpensive roller shade treated with a fusible adhesive. Just trim a map and iron it in place! How-to instructions begin on page 226.

**another idea:** Cover a shade with another paper item, such as an old poster or leftover wallpaper. Or use fabric to match your room decor.

# window hardware

These little details can make a
big fashion statement.

## 172
## a little sparkle

Don't be shy about mixing materials and textures when dressing your
windows. The distressed finish of a painted rod and rings contrasts
nicely with shiny chandelier crystals attached to the rings. Look for
embellishments such as costume jewelry, old buttons, or keys, which
can be stitched easily onto plain drapery hardware.

# 73
## new country

Country panels take on a new look when hung from a peg rack of crystal doorknobs. Large buttonholes make it easy to slip the panels in place. How-to instructions begin on page 226.

# 74
## hats off

When you're not wearing a hat, you can still show it off. This collection of straw hats becomes a whimsical valance, adding outdoor appeal to the porch. **another idea:** In a child's bedroom, fashion a valance from baseball caps to play up a sporting theme. Think beyond hats to other collections or interests, too. Vintage handbags, pennants hung vertically, doll clothes—with a little imagination, you may already have a novel valance at your fingertips.

# 75
## piping hot

Double layers of sheer fabric edged in piping fall in graceful tassel-tipped points. Purchased tiebacks mounted above the window frame hold the valance in place. Look for such hardware at drapery and home decorating stores, or substitute cabinet knobs, doorknobs, or similar decorative items.

How-to instructions begin on page 226.

## midas touch

Curtain tiebacks needn't be expensive to be sophisticated. The tieback on the bathroom window at *left* consists of a wooden screw-in ball finial, available in home centers and drapery departments. Paint the wooden ball gold and adorn it with metallic-tone tassels. The sheers were run-of-the-mill white cotton panels until randomly stenciled stars made them shine. **another idea:** Use finials to hold back a shower curtain.

# 76

# 77
## bamboo beauty

Look beyond manufactured hardware when hanging draperies. With understated elegance, a bamboo pole, *above*, becomes a rod resting on doorknob brackets. The antique glass knobs attach to the wall with long, double-end screws.

# 78

## express yourself

Use your favorite expression to hang your curtains for a light, friendly look. Attach brass letters to your walls with hooks and suspend the drapery panels.

# 79
## nautical nights

Turn an antique oar into a curtain rod, or buy a new one and paint it. Fashion curtains from map-print fabric and punch metal grommets at the top. Lace the panels with rope to hang them from the oar.

# 80
## sign of the times

Napkins and napkin rings decorate a window for the season. It takes only a few minutes to change the linens and rings as the holidays, special occasions, or your moods change.
How-to instructions begin on page 226.

# 81
## hook it

Skip installing a curtain rod—use a row of iron hooks instead. Place the hooks about 6 inches apart and attach sheers with pretty ribbons looped around the hooks. Use your imagination when searching for hardware—decorative brackets or doorknobs are just as fun.

82

## wrapped in style

If you naturally gravitate toward neutrals and solid colors, you still have plenty of options for adding visual interest. Narrow grosgrain ribbon wrapped around wooden curtain rings can make an up-high pattern play. We made eight wraps around each drapery ring, tying each ribbon in a square knot at the base of its ring. This little dose of detailing gives a big impact.

# containers
## for all

When it comes to showing off flowers and other treasures, don't limit yourself. Go all out!

 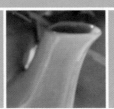  

# 83
# buttons and bouquets

Turn your button collection into a flower frog to show off an arrangement of fresh, silk, or dried flowers.

84

## creative containers

For fresh-flower bouquets, the most interesting ones often are homespun, not the perfect arrangements that come from the florist. After you pluck flowers—whether a few buds or a dozen blooms—from your garden, slip them into containers that are at your fingertips to create whimsical bouquets. Fill a teapot from a child's play set with miniature roses, *above left*, or use a grown-up teapot that has lost its lid, *left*. Even an old enamelware coffeepot, *above*, is a worthy candidate.

Almost anything that can hold water—from durable metals to fine china—can become a charming vase. Use buckets, cans, or jars alone, or group them in a flat-bottom basket or on a serving tray. You'll be pleasantly surprised by these everyday charmers.

# 85
## campfire retreat

An old enamel coffeepot that spent its younger years on the trail retires to a place of honor on the kitchen table. A simply painted plaid design provides the necessary face-lift.
How-to instructions begin on page 226.

# 86
## yipes, stripes!

Painted awning-style stripes brighten a galvanized tub—a playful way to hold flowers, ice, or beverages.
How-to instructions begin on page 226.

# 88
## weaved wire

Covered with wire, a clear-glass vase takes on textural interest. How-to instructions begin on page 226.

# 87
## abracadabra!

Make your arrangements magical by filling a short container with flowers and hiding it inside a top hat (or any flat-top hat). To give the flowers extra support, scrunch a 12-inch square of chicken wire into the container or jar. The wire makes arranging the flowers easier and holds them upright.

# 89
## plant
## an idea

Use bedding plants inside before putting them in your garden. Place violas, pansies, and other annuals (still in their original containers) in an assortment of cheese boxes, berry baskets, or similar holders to create a tabletop garden.

## under glass

Flea market finds may not be priceless pieces, but they're treasures just the same. Put on a glass pedestal, everyday items will be seen in a whole new light. Hose nozzles, glass blocks, and a clock reveal new beauty when they go under covers. While hunting for your "collectibles," look for glass plates, trays, or cake pedestals to team with bell jars or cake domes. Don't worry about finding matching pieces—these one-of-a-kind discoveries team up just fine.

## perfect chemistry

The beakers you loved to hate in chemistry class can work wonders out of the classroom. For a sparkling display, group different styles and sizes of the glass containers, and fill them with colored glass chips, sprigs of ivy, and flowers. Bring a gazing ball designed for the outdoors into the home to add more luster. If you have problems finding beakers, check with a nearby school for a source.

## 92 up against the fence

Galvanized pots from the hardware store or garden center take a dip in Popsicle-bright colors. Hang them in a row from the fence or use them as centerpieces.
How-to instructions begin on page 226.

## 93 pull up a seat

Garden guests will sit up and take notice when they see an old chair with a flower box seat. Look for chairs with missing cushions and seats; then build a simple box to hold the flowers.
How-to instructions begin on page 226.

# marvelous
## moldings

Moldings pack plenty of personality
for little cost and effort.

94

# out on a ledge

Wide crown moldings yield the perfect platforms for displaying shallow objects, such as photographs, plates, vases, and knickknacks. Boards are cut to fit just below the top edge to hold displays securely. How-to instructions begin on page 226.

## 95 shake things up

Shaker pegs ring this room at varying heights, acting as hangers for the curtains as well as the photographs. Capped with a shelf, they provide added display space.

## 96 console yourself

Install an architectural sideboard, console, or buffet with corbels topped with a narrow shelf. Vintage brackets can be found in antiques shops and salvage houses; reproductions are available at home improvement centers.

How-to instructions begin on page 226.

## 97 high and dry

Keep your stemware safe and close at hand by using exposed racks. The crystal will add a bit of sparkle to the wall, especially when highlighted by candlelight on the shelves above.

How-to instructions begin on page 226.

# faux facade 98

Replicate a built-in hutch with windowsill, colonial casing, and standard pieces.
Using the same wallpaper below the chair rail and within the plate rack further
carries out the look of a built-in.

How-to instructions begin on page 226.

# 99 divide & conquer

Break up a long, tall wall with vertical and horizontal strips. Screen molding divides the wall into vertical panels, and a custom molding tops the panels to make the wall appear shorter.

How-to instructions begin on page 226.

# 100
## top it off

Cap a window with a shelf to display your favorite collections. Tension rods between the purchased brackets hold the window treatment in place.

How-to instructions begin on page 226.

# 101
## framed!

These kids have been framed! A kitchen soffit lined with cherry trim and cork backing is the perfect display place for school photos. What a great way to track the kids' growth.

How-to instructions begin on page 226.

# unusual
# tables

Webster may soon have to change his definition of "table." Today, almost any object that **safely holds** your necessities can function as a table.

# 102
## stepping out

Even with nicks and peeling paint, a small stepladder topped with a lace doily makes a charming plant stand. Bring in color with bright blooms and containers, or go for the natural look with weathered clay pots. Rag rugs and a watering can are right in step with the ladder.

# 103
## form and function

This table rides the line between practical and sculptural. Four large landscape finials form the base for the glass top, creating a modern art accessory. How-to instructions begin on page 226.

# 104
## excess baggage

If you can't find the perfect end table, head to the nearest flea market and look for old suitcases in graduated sizes. They look great and can store seldom-used items.
How-to instructions begin on page 226.

# 105
## gingerbread cutout

Cookie-cutter pretty, this tabletop requires advanced woodworking skills, but the results will be well worth it. How-to instructions begin on page 226.

# 106
## getting benched

Old wooden wash benches, step stools, and narrow seating pieces often can be found in basements, garages, or flea markets. Stack several together for a graphic effect. How-to instructions begin on page 226.

## luggage rack 107

Once bound for glory, two vintage suitcases now are homeward bound as a functional side table that offers storage for books, toys, or out-of-season clothing. Stack 'em two or three at a time to get the desired height, then place a bouquet of flowers or a reading lamp on top.

## 108 primary desires

Give your bench some pizzazz with paint swatches in primary colors. Paint an unfinished bench with two or three layers of a base color, sanding lightly between coats. Arrange paint cards in an eye-catching sequence, trimming if necessary. Spray-glue the cards in place. Finish with a coat (or more) of polyurethane.

## 109 laptop display

Placed atop a larger table, a lap table designed for writing creates an extra level for an artful exhibit. Antique glass remedy bottles add sparkle and double as vases for fresh flowers. Below the lap table, a stack of books adds more decorative charm and easy-to-reach reading material.

## delightful array

Showcase your favorite pictures, stamps, buttons, or artwork under glass. Have two pieces of glass cut to fit your table. Set one piece of glass into the table frame, arrange your collection, and rest the other piece of glass on top for a shadow-box effect.

**110**

**111**

## clothespin craze

Accent a bedside table with a skirt of clothespins for a look that's wash-line fresh.

**tip:** Clothespins in the same package may vary slightly in size, are not always perfectly shaped, and may split when nailed. Buy extra so you have enough for your project.

How-to instructions begin on page 226.

# pretty pillows

Wake up any space with these ideas, which will have friends and family abuzz with pillow talk.

 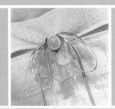  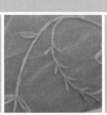

# 112 | patio pick-me-ups

Sporting fun fabrics, buttons, and rickrack, a trio of patio pillows becomes a cheerful plump-up for outdoor furniture. Choose durable and affordable materials, such as terry cloth, cotton knit, and piqué. Dressmaker details, such as rickrack, ribbon, and button trims, provide the finishing touches. These indoor-outdoor pillows are such a snap to make, you'll have plenty of time to sit back and enjoy an ice-cold drink.

How-to instructions begin on page 226.

# spring greens

The staples you need to make this spring-fresh ensemble may be as close as your kitchen drawer or pantry. With a few coordinating towels and the help of a potato, you'll be on your way to a creative pillow display for a bed. The small white boudoir pillow is made from a single hand towel; the green stripe pillow is fashioned from two dish towels sewn together and embellished with daisy buttons. To tie the look together, the edge of a white pillowcase was stamped with a potato carved with a design and dipped into paint.

How-to instructions begin on page 226.

114

# rickrack reunion

If you want to turn on the charm, just reach for the rickrack. The nifty, thrifty trim has been around for years, and it keeps getting better. We used a mix of summery fabrics and the most common sizes of rickrack—baby, medium, and jumbo—to add homespun flair to the comfy pillows at *left*.

How-to instructions begin on page 226.

**another idea:** Dress up plain hand towels and washcloths by sewing rickrack along the bottom or in the banding.

# a mark above

Leave your mark with a monogram pillow. You don't have to be a needlework whiz when you start with a vintage handkerchief that already has an embroidered monogram. Hankies, which have become collector's items, sport many colorful and whimsical designs that transition nicely to charming accent pillows.

How-to instructions begin on page 226.

**another idea:** Use a vintage dresser scarf (fold or cut as desired) or pillowcase for an easy, nearly no-sew pillow.

115

# 116
## all dressed up

Dig out old shirts from the back of your closet and use them to create buttoned-up pillows. When the pillowcases need to be cleaned, simply unbutton the covers and add them to the family laundry.

How-to instructions begin on page 226.

# 117

## grandma's embroidery

Recycle tea towels, napkins, and aprons that Grandma spent hours embroidering to make vintage pillows. Showcase the embroidered designs, decorative edgings, and even pockets, then use antique buttons for a final flourish. How-to instructions begin on page 226.

# 118
## white wonders

The trick to getting white right is to mix shades—from bright white to cream and taupe—and texture. Layer crisp white organza over oatmeal-colored linen pillows and embellish with buttons or sew-ons for a decorative touch.

# 119
## sweet dreams

Bedtime is more fun when you cuddle up with a special pillow. To help your children personalize theirs, purchase pillowcases and dye sticks. Use the sticks, available at crafts stores, to draw a design on a pillowcase, working in small sections. After finishing one section of the design, cover it with a sheet of paper and press with a hot iron to set the dye. This prevents smudging as you continue to work. Draw and color, covering each newly completed section with paper and ironing until the design is complete.

## four square

Sewing high-style accent pillows can be amazingly simple. The secret is to match fabrics—silk, satin, or synthetic suede, for example—with dressmaking details such as appliqué or pleating. How-to instructions begin on page 226.

120

# one-hour pillows

Making a case for fabulous pillows is easy with any of these quick-as-a-wink creative ideas.

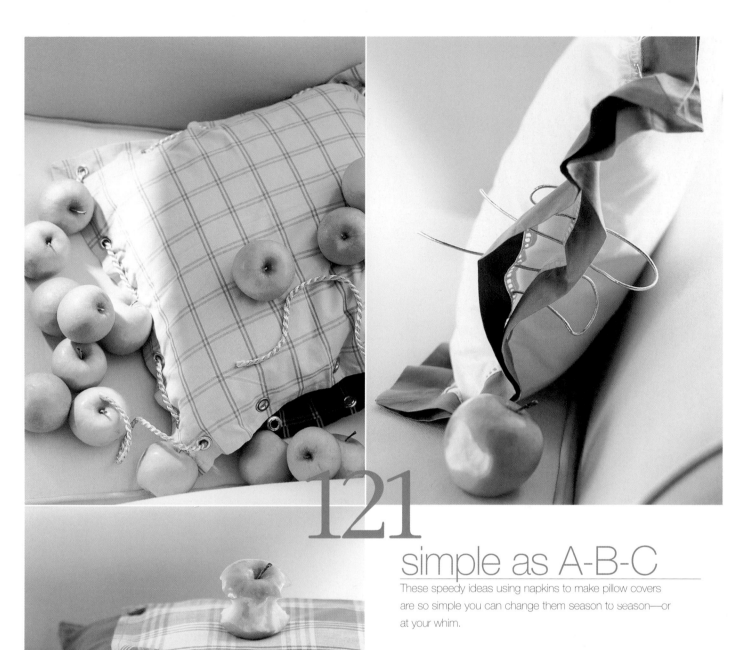

# 121

## simple as A-B-C

These speedy ideas using napkins to make pillow covers are so simple you can change them season to season—or at your whim.

Using grommets and cording, lace two napkins over a pillow form to come together in a jiffy, *above left*. Use two matching napkins, or mix colors or patterns to reverse the pillow.

Some napkins have already-existing openings for lacing. Sash together openwork on the edges for a pillow cover, *above*.

Add a dash of pattern by buttoning a cocktail napkin over a plain pillow, *left*. Use a purchased pillow or make a cover from a pair of dinner napkins.

How-to instructions begin on page 226.

# a way with
# walls

Revamp weary walls with
pleasing paints, artful wallpaper,
and beckoning borders.
Your walls won't just talk, they'll sing!

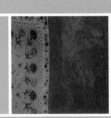

# fabric treatments

Dress your walls in fabrics, and they're sure to make a **stylish** statement.

# 122

## checkerboard charm

Triple-jump your walls to a winning look with a checkerboard wainscot. Paste squares of two complementary fabrics to the wall with wallpaper adhesive. Careful measuring is key: Divide the distance between the chair rail and baseboard molding into even portions; cut the fabric squares to fit. Do not butt fabric up to the molding; this allows the wall color to show through and defines the grid pattern. Keep cut fabric from unraveling by pressing gently around the edges of the squares.

# classic panels

For extra texture, softness, and flexibility, outfit your walls in fabric. These panels are 54-inch-wide decorator fabric pieces with a large, repeated motif on one width of the fabric, which works best because you use less yardage. Divide the fabric lengthwise and use one half for each panel. Apply the fabric as you would nonprepasted wallpaper using wallpaper adhesive. Hide the edges with strips of painted molding for a finished look.

**123**

# 124

## powder room pizzazz

Billowing sheets give this bathroom exotic flair. The fabric is dramatic, but doesn't make the room look too dark.

### START TO FINISH

STEP 1. Buy enough bed sheets to cover 1½ times each wall's width.

STEP 2. Cut the sheets to fit from floor to ceiling, leaving small hems intact for use as a top casing.

STEP 3. Shirr sheets onto narrow curtain rods, slitting hems to insert rods. Hang rods where the wall and ceiling join. To finish off the bottom, turn under the raw edge to butt baseboard; finger-pleat and staple to wall.

STEP 4. For the vanity skirt, cut enough fabric to fit 1½ times the front and side measurements. Hem and softly gather the top edge; hem the bottom. Attach the skirt's upper edge with hook-and-loop tape.

# go to
# great depths

Take walls beyond the flat-paint look with techniques that add feeling and texture.

125

# 126
## rag time

The multidimensional look of this wall was achieved with an aptly named "ragging off" technique. Paint walls with a satin base coat (we used a pale lavender); let dry. Mix a darker shade of the satin base coat with glaze. Working in a section of about two roller widths, roll the glaze mixture onto the wall. With a clean, dry rag, blot the glaze, removing some of it and taking care not to blot to the edge of the rolled glaze. Repeat the rolling and blotting process. To blend edges, rag off the seams. Clean, dry rags are a must; a saturated rag won't remove the glaze.

## plate it up

Not at the dining table, but on your walls! With dinner plate in hand, you're ready to create a stencil for a mottled-circle design like the one *opposite*. Trace around the plate onto poster board, cut out the center of the circle, and tape the stencil to the wall. Apply paint to a piece of clear acetate, then press the acetate onto the wall in the stencil's center to create the mottled circles.

How-to instructions begin on page 226.

**another idea:** Adapt the technique to other simple shapes, such as squares or diamonds.

# 127

# 128

# 129

## 127 flower power

For walls that really blossom, add blooms of your own. Dauber sponges used for stenciling and stamping are easy to cut into shapes. To create a design like this, fashion a large dauber into petals and cut a small one to form the center.

How-to instructions begin on page 226.

## 128 do the polka

Stamp out boredom with daubers that form irregular polka dots. Snipping away pieces from the center and outer edge results in an arty design from a plain round shape.

How-to instructions begin on page 226.

## 129 on a roll

For professional-looking faux-finish walls without the cost, become a faux designer for a day. A host of clever new paint tools and kits makes it possible, and proves that everything is easier when you have the proper equipment. For the marbled, plasterlike effect on the dining room wall at *right*, we chose the Italianate pattern from Wagner's WallMagic Designer Series. Winding streams carved into 5-inch foam rollers create the textural design. Dip the double roller into the divided paint tray in the kit and simultaneously roll on dual colors (we used a pale blue and a medium delphinium blue). Look for decorative paint tools and kits, available for less than $50, at home centers and paint stores.

# paper chase

Your walls will make headlines of their own
with the right choices in prints.

## 130
## spice
## is nice

Add unforgettable flavor to your
kitchen walls with designs on seed
packets, old advertisements, or
small posters and prints.
How-to instructions begin on
page 226.

# 131
## high ambitions

Photocopies from a vintage botanicals book bring a graceful English garden look to a small powder room. The "frames" are photocopies of one drawn by an artist, then reproduced to fit around each print. How-to instructions begin on page 226.

**132**

# looking 'tile-ish'

Create the knockout look of tile without the work or expense
by framing a mirror with photocopied images. Run a row at
chair-rail height, then border the entire design with braid.
How-to instructions begin on page 226.

# 133

## great rotation

To update artwork frequently and easily, suspend favorite finds from decorative knobs attached to a runner. Hang from a set height so pieces can be replaced without hammering new holes.

# 134
## big-time results

Large-scale blossoms make a great first impression in a small entryway. For designs as big as these, use full-size posters from art stores or online sources. Border the prints with coordinated grosgrain ribbon.
How-to instructions begin on page 226.

# 135
## worldly walls

No need to spend hours flipping through wallpaper books in search of the right pattern. Map prints photocopied from an 1876 geography book are casually tacked to the wall above a desk for an intriguing wall covering. **another idea:** Use the same concept to create a theme that suits you or your family. Think beyond the pages from books. Vintage seed packets can grace the wall of a potting shed, and photocopied family recipes in Grandmother's handwriting can recall fond memories when displayed in the kitchen.

## timeless nature

Art clipped from calendars and books and applied to walls decoupage-style will give a kitchen or bath an old-world look. Polyurethane seals and protects the display from water damage.

# 136

# a shoe-in

Get your closet in step with shoe prints marching smartly across the wall. Decorative upholstery tacks form distinctive frames when equally spaced around pictures. After you've "framed" the pictures, add wallpaper borders for an added sense of order in an often disorderly space. To change the design, simply remove the glued-on prints as you would wallpaper.

137

# geometry
# lessons

Deciding on the perfect wall treatment often
is a matter of conjuring up the right angle.

# 138
## all that glitters

Iridescent squares created from spray-painted
stencils will float like bubbles on a wall. Look for
appropriate spray paints at paint, crafts, and
decorating stores. Avoid paints intended for
metal finishes.

How-to instructions begin on page 226.

## 139

### freehand

These lines don't quite follow the straight and narrow. Because they're painted freehand, they shimmy a little and give the design interest and movement.

How-to instructions begin on page 226.

## 140

### stripe it rich

Deep colors and a sandy texture add luxurious allure to this wall. Textured paint catches the light—in contrast to flat surfaces. Look for such paints at paint and home improvement stores.

How-to instructions begin on page 226.

### check things out

You'll really be cooking with a checkerboard kitchen wall that mimics the look of tile or wallpaper and a complementary border. Best of all, no time-consuming taping off is required; the free-form style befits the room's casual cottage style. You'll need only a measuring tape and a level to keep the rows straight. The checks can go as high or as low on the wall as you want. For a mottled look and to add depth to the checks, sponge off some of the paint as you work, or add glaze to the paint.

How-to instructions begin on page 226.

## 141

## 142 friends finale

Diamonds are a decorator's best friend. Large renditions in different colors are applied with a glaze, and then a sheer glaze is rolled over the top to soften the effect.

How-to instructions begin on page 226.

## 143 three's a charm

Can't decide on just one decorative paint technique? This stripes-and-leaves wall is a stylish mix of three techniques. Wide stripes, a faux-linen finish, and stenciled leaves create the classy ensemble. Paint the base coat, then tape off the stripes (ours are 24 inches wide). Mix a lighter hue of the base-coat color with glaze, and use a linen paintbrush to apply it to alternating stripes to create the linen finish. For the final touch, nothing beats stencils. Though the ginkgo-leaf stencil was intended for an overall effect, we used it to give the look of leaves falling off a tree.

How-to instructions begin on page 226.

## 144 grid works

Create a grid with low-tack painter's tape. A special roller automatically blends the colors for a softly marbled appearance.

How-to instructions begin on page 226.

# 145
## look-alikes

Used in small doses, fool-the-eye papers that mimic marble, leather, or fine woodgrain make big statements. This stone-look paper is rolled on and framed with a narrow wallpaper border that resembles architectural trim, adding three-dimensional interest to the room.

# 146

## hip to be square

When stumped for ideas on how to punch up a white wall, let a room's fabric pieces serve as inspiration. The bedding launched this color-block treatment featuring five pastel hues. Paint a base coat (we used yellow), and let dry. Along two dominant walls, use a level and pencil to mark squares. To calculate the size of the squares, measure the wall height and divide by two. With painter's tape, mark off the squares that will be one color. Paint the tape edges with matte medium, available at art supply stores, to prevent bleeding; let dry. Roll the desired hue in the squares, and remove the tape. Let dry before painting the adjacent squares. Repeat the process with the remaining colors.

# 147 dazzling diamonds

Turn boring walls into brilliant creations with easy sponge painting. To jazz up your walls with a textured design like this, tape off diamonds and gently sponge light brown paint over a blue base.

# creative
# ceilings

Overhead treatments can have things
really looking up while adding character
and covering flaws.

## 148

# land of wonder

Let your child live a fairy-tale life with Alice, the Mad Hatter, and the White Rabbit peeking down from the ceiling. Paint the mural on canvas and adhere it to the ceiling with wallpaper paste. Once the theme is outgrown, remove the canvas and use it as an area rug in your home.

# 149
## center of attention

Embossed wallpaper and a matching border impart the look of expensive plasterwork at the center of this ceiling. High-quality embossed paper is available at wallpaper and decorating stores, and less expensive versions can now be found at home improvement centers.

How-to instructions begin on page 226.

# 150
## by design

Hit the jackpot with a design that not only adds interest but also makes a narrow room look a bit wider. These three painted diamonds have a faux finish applied with a wallpaper brush.
How-to instructions begin on page 226.

# 151
## a perfect tin

Tin is in, but old ceiling tins can be expensive and hard to find. Get the same look with embossed wallpaper. Cover the ceiling to add textural interest; then extend a band down onto the wall and finish it with a row of molding. How-to instructions begin on page 226.

# 152
## high marks

Emphasize a chandelier with arrangements of molding, creating the same effect as framing a work of art. The rows of molding are progressively narrower, and the colors change with each band.
How-to instructions begin on page 226.

# outdoor looks indoors

Follow Mother Nature's cue with these garden-inspired ideas for your home, patio, or porch. No green thumb required!

# indoor turf 153

The lush lawn you've longed for just got more manageable.
Create a one-of-a-kind look by placing a mat of wheat grass in
an old berry basket. First, line the basket with foil; then insert
the wheat grass, typically available from florists. Look for berry
baskets or other flat wooden crates at antiques stores and
flea markets. **another idea:** Experiment with different grasses
that have interesting colors and textures to create unusual
displays. Ornamental grasses, for example, make intriguing
indoor potted displays.

## 154

## inside out

Scour your yard, garage, and potting shed, and then drag favorite outdoor elements inside for a surprising decorating twist. At *left,* a large urn becomes a great resting place for magazines or newspapers. Ornamental grasses and a stack of rocks in a birdbath create a living sculpture. Elsewhere, towering ornamental grasses fill empty spaces and add design drama. Don't fret about the weathered appearance of urns, pots, or birdbaths—it only adds to the natural beauty.

## for the birds

Fun and functional, the birdbath table *opposite* is sure to get guests chirping. The glass top offers a handy display surface and acts as a lid to safely encase mementos (see inset photo *opposite*). Purchase a vintage or new birdbath—inexpensive terra-cotta and cast-concrete birdbaths are available at nurseries and home centers. If desired, you can age them by rubbing on water-diluted latex paint. Fill the bowl with river rocks, shells, seed balls, or marbles; then add seed packets, old photos, postcards, gardening tools, or other items you want to display. Cover the birdbath with a glass top $\frac{1}{2}$ inch thick. A 24-inch-diameter circle works well for an average-size birdbath. For stability and safety, glue the bowl and base together with silicon adhesive.

## bookmarks 156

Two of the best bargains in decorating? Old books and seashells. Books will encourage browsing and can serve as a pedestal to display favorite objects, such as shells. Stack an odd number of books that have colorful spines and covers to complement your decor, and then top with a basket. **another idea:** Marbles and vintage postcards make interesting ideas for the basket contents.

155

# fall flair

Recycle old picture frames to create stylish serving trays that feature leaf collages preserved under glass.

START TO FINISH

STEP 1. Remove the solid back from the frame. Paint frame and two screen-door handles with gold acrylic paint. Let dry; then brush surfaces with an antiquing mixture, removing some with a sponge. Spray the frame and handles with matte sealer.

STEP 2. Cut two pieces of glass or clear plastic as needed to fit the frame. Turn frame upside down. Insert one piece of glass or plastic into frame.

STEP 3. Arrange pressed leaves, colorful side down, on top of the glass. Position smaller leaves near the outside and larger leaves near the center, filling the surface.

STEP 4. Place the second piece of glass or plastic over the first, using glazing points to hold it in place. Screw 1- to-1½-inch molding into place on the back of the frame. Attach handles to the outside of the frame.

# 158
# herbal remedy

Go for the unexpected at your next dinner party. Instead of a floral centerpiece, bring a touch of Tuscany to your table with fresh herbs that overflow from stacked pots. Sprigs of parsley, sage, and rosemary come together to form a fragrant herbal centerpiece that resembles greenery tumbling over rocks on an Italian hillside. Grow your own herbs, or buy them at a grocery store, nursery, or farmer's market. Water the centerpiece for several days of freshness, or let the sprigs go dry for an everlasting arrangement.

How-to instructions begin on page 226.

# 159

## terra-cotta transformation

With an easy-to-do bas-relief technique, plain terra-cotta pots become striking sculptures. Using leaves and seedpods for the design, concrete for the texture, and paint for the burnished patina, bas-relief pots will blossom into intriguing art indoors or out. Make these pots in complementary or contrasting colors; then fill with your favorite plants or give them as gifts to gardeners.
How-to instructions begin on page 226.

# 160
## roll with it

A wheelbarrow topped with a piece of glass becomes a fashionable and affordable coffee table. Add favorite memorabilia, sand, and tools, or leave it empty. Adhere felt furniture pads, available at home centers, to the bottom of the metal legs to protect floors and carpeting.
**another idea:** When hosting a party, use the wheelbarrow as a cooler. Remove the top and memorabilia; then fill the wheelbarrow with ice.

# 161
## cascade effect

Graceful grasses drape over the edge of a box mounted under shutter-style windows, creating a cozy continental atmosphere.

How-to instructions begin on page 226.

# 163

# 162

## points well taken

Pickets form the wainscot and window box in this room,
spreading garden-fresh charm throughout.
How-to instructions begin on page 226.

## blooming tales

Scalloped brackets support a garden center window
box, and flowering plants add color and softness
to the window lines. Ivy, croton, cyclamen, and
kalanchoe are great choices for indoor planters.
How-to instructions begin on page 226.

# bedroom
## beauty
## lifts

Bored with your bed? Long to slumber in style? These beautiful backdrops and cocooning canopies make any bed a real dream.

# architectural
## appeal
### To add elements of style to any headboard, seek out items that offer allure.

164

## rescue operation

One great piece of salvage can add immeasurable character to a plain bedroom. Look
for old finials, door toppers, or even a mantel that will fit above your bed. Be patient. It may
take a while to find just the right piece.

How-to instructions begin on page 226.

# 165
## garden bed

Give a country garden look to an ordinary bed frame, *below*. Preassembled stockade fencing from a home improvement store can easily be trimmed and painted to create the look of an indoor garden. For stability, the tall frame is anchored to the wall instead of the bed.

How-to instructions begin on page 226.

# 166
## door to door

The handsome paneled headboard *above* is really a wooden door turned on its side. To make it, buy a six-panel door with no hole for a doorknob. For the bedside shelves, purchase a circular tabletop with a routed edge. Cut the tabletop into quarters (or have a home center do it for you). Screw a table quarter to each bottom corner of the headboard. Attach a decorative bracket below the shelf. Screw a 1×4 board along the top edge of the headboard, and use finishing nails to attach a molding strip where the 1×4 meets the door. Paint or finish the headboard as desired, and screw it to the wall studs at the desired height.

# 167
## overnight frame

Old tin ceiling panels—from flea markets, salvage stores, antiques shops, or torn-down buildings—offer instant architecture to a room filled with unusual objects. If large panels are unavailable, substitute several rows of small tins.
How-to instructions begin on page 226.

# 168
## au naturel headboard

Easily create a rustic headboard with materials from your own backyard. Tie twigs and branches together and attach the headboard to the wall with hooks. If you grow tired of the look, it will be quick to disassemble.

# fabric
# headboards

Weave sensational sleep surroundings with
this tapestry of ideas.

169

## fabric frame-up

Even if you're not an artist, you can paint a pretty picture in your bedroom
with this idea: Stretch a piece of fabric over an artist's canvas, and hang
it on the wall to create a headboard. We chose the lavender flower print
for its painterly effect, but simple stripes or warm plaids would work just
as well. To finish the canvas headboard, glue coordinating gimp or ribbon
around the outside edge. Ready-made canvases, which give lightweight
fabrics a firm backing, are available at art supply stores in standard sizes
(ours is 42 inches).

How-to instructions begin on page 226.

# 170
## under cover

Soften the appearance of a headboard with a no-sew cover-up. Cut a sheet 2 inches wider than the top of your headboard and long enough to drape over the front and back. (For this project, a twin sheet made it even easier since it only had to be turned on its side to make the cover-up.) Press under the raw edges and fuse in place with iron-on hemming tape. Accent with tied ribbons to hold the fabric in place.

# 171

## cushy comfort

Prop yourself against a comfortable padded headboard made of thick foam. With a zip-off cover for easy cleaning, this soft backing eliminates the need for high-maintenance piles of pillows. To secure the headboard in place, loop fabric over decorative drawer knobs anchored into the wall.

172

# flower shower

For a no-sew canopy, tack a shower curtain on the wall behind a bed. We capitalized on the holes or grommets that shower curtains have along the top edge and used drawer knobs to suspend the canopy. Not only is it a snap to hang, but the treatment takes the place of artwork above a headboard. **another idea:** Buy an additional shower curtain to make pillows. After you get the drama up high, bring it down to floor level with a bed skirt made from a coordinating sheet. How-to instructions begin on page 226.

## quilt rack

Turn a pretty quilt into a homespun headboard. Cut a wooden drapery rod slightly longer than the width of the bed. Add a finial to each end of the rod. Hang from brackets anchored into the wall. Fold the quilt over the rod. Use brass quilters' safety pins, which won't rust or leave stains, to pin both sides of the quilt together under the rod, securing on the inside edges.

173

174

## upright position

Never again will the pillows droop and flop when you read in bed. These large squares hang from a curtain rod so they will always be in the right place at the right time. How-to instructions begin on page 226.

# fantastic canopies

Your bedroom's fashion statement definitely
will be on a higher plane with these tips.

## 175
## bargain beauty

Surrounding yourself in luxury is easy—yet need not break the bank.
For a canopy design like this, use inexpensive edging fabric and ties from
a discount store, and splurge on stylish sheets for the fabric panels.
Assemble 1×2 lumber into a bed-size rectangular frame, and suspend
it from the ceiling.

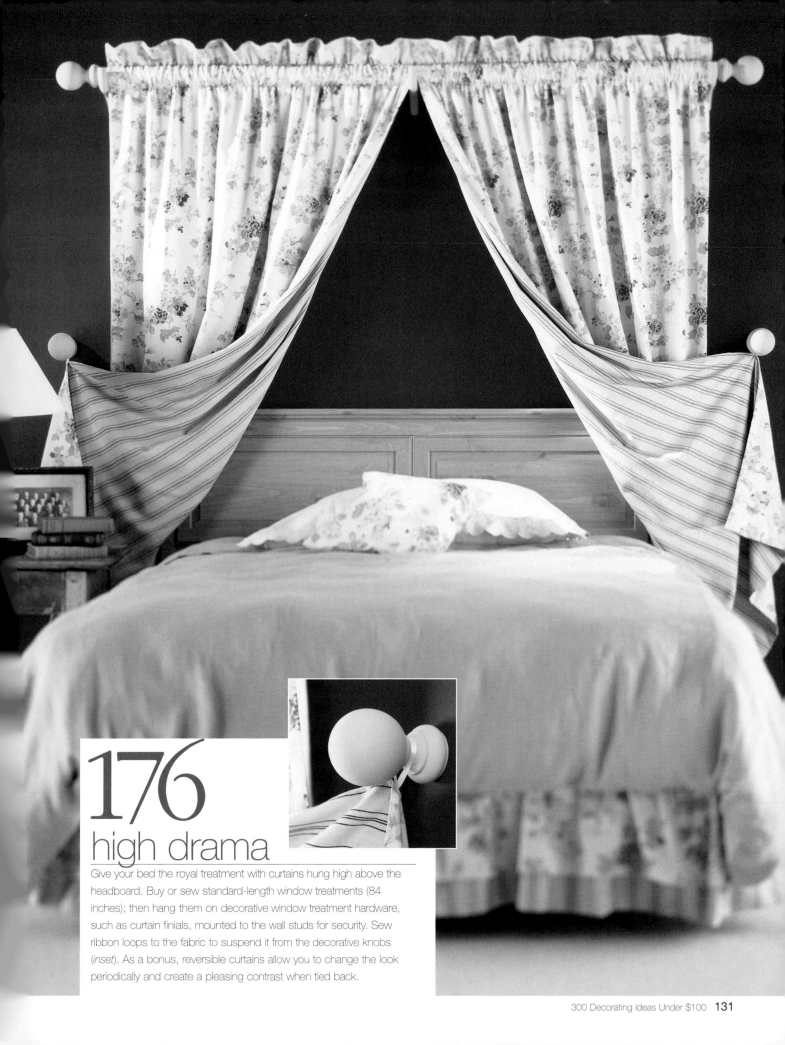

# 176
## high drama

Give your bed the royal treatment with curtains hung high above the headboard. Buy or sew standard-length window treatments (84 inches); then hang them on decorative window treatment hardware, such as curtain finials, mounted to the wall studs for security. Sew ribbon loops to the fabric to suspend it from the decorative knobs (*inset*). As a bonus, reversible curtains allow you to change the look periodically and create a pleasing contrast when tied back.

## sheer bliss

# 177

Like a bride's veil, this sheer canopy adds a final flourish to a pure and pretty bedroom. The filmy fabric is a perfect counterpoint to the nubby chenille bedspread. To make the canopy, center a white scarf sconce, available at curtain retailers, over your bed. Thread 6 yards of inexpensive sheer fabric through the holder and fan out behind the bed, draping the fabric edges over the frame.

# 178
## sleek retreat

Chrome towel rings and sheer fabric frame a bed in easy, breezy style. Requiring only two small holes, the canopy also keeps ceilings virtually unmarred. Mount the towel rings to the ceiling at the outer points of the bed. (Measure your bed width first; then mark the width on the ceiling.) Hem the ends of a length of sheer gauzy fabric (we used 8 yards), and loop the fabric through the rings.

# 179
## twin set

A crowning canopy will give a twin bed big presence. Mount a half-moon-shape metal corona to the wall 6 inches from the ceiling, centering it above the bed. Use an extralong, full-size flat sheet for a soft backdrop. Fold 2½ inches at the foot of the sheet to the wrong side. Sew close to the prefinished edge to make a top rod pocket. For the side panels, use 54-inch-wide fabric. To determine the length, measure from the top of the corona to the floor; and add 9 inches. To finish the side edges, press under ½ inch, then 1½ inches. Sew close to the first fold. For the top rod pocket, press under ½ inch, then 5 inches. Sew across the panel close to the first fold. Sew again 2 inches above the first seam. Slide the panel onto the corona; mark the hem. Press under ½ inch, then at the hem marking; sew in place. Repeat for the second panel.

## four-poster flair

Bring romance to the bedroom with a four-poster fashioned from fabric. Lengths of lightweight fabric hung through circular finials formed the restful retreat at *left* in just minutes. You'll need four finials with accompanying hardware that can be screwed into the ceiling. To determine the finial placement, tie a pencil or small weight to the end of a string. At each corner of the bed, dangle the string from the ceiling so the weighted end clears the corners of the bed; mark the place on the ceiling, allowing for the fullness of the fabric to skim the floor or fall into puddles. Attach the finials to the ceiling. Drape the fabric through the finials to form a rectangle at the top, or cross the lengths in the center.

180

## net gain

Wrap a few yards of delicate fabric loosely around the top of your bed frame for an ethereal look. Check your local fabric store for tulle or mosquito netting with finished edges.

181

## 182
## arbor day

When updating your bedroom, head to the garden department of a home improvement store. Ready-made or easy-to-assemble trellises and arbors are available in a variety of sizes and styles. Measure the bed and ceiling to ensure a good fit. How-to instructions begin on page 226.

# 183
## tubular magic

PVC pipe forms the frame for a canopy of sheets.
Coordinating patterns cut from twin-size sheets are sewn
into one long strip. The lightweight pipe and canopy can
be installed with minimal wall damage. The canopy is
easily removed for routine cleaning.

How-to instructions begin on page 226.

# fanciful floors

Perform incredible feats of magic with faux runners and coordinating rugs that will impress every step of the way.

 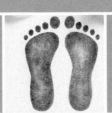  

# raving about rugs

To spruce up any room, all you have to do is look underfoot.

# 184
## throw them a curve

Soften a hard-angled room with a floor that welcomes all who enter with a friendly wave. Undulating edges and different colors of carpeting in this room lead the eye on a exciting path in what otherwise would be a straight-and-narrow design journey. Position furniture appropriately along the well-chosen path.

# 185

## show your stripes

Liven up wood floors with a lightweight cotton throw rug. Purchase six 24×48-inch rugs with stripes in various hues. Cut the rugs in half to form 24-inch squares; then piece their raw edges together with the stripes running in opposite directions. Using a sewing machine, carpet thread, and a size 16 or 18 needle, stitch a row of three squares together with 5⁄16-inch seams. Repeat for the other rows and stitch the rows together. Press all seams flat.

# 186
## tapestry dance

For a no-sew showstopper, layer two fabrics and then bind them together with iron-on adhesive. For the tapestry rug at *left,* we framed a piece of ornate fabric with a solid-color border. The adhesive, available in 18-inch widths and strips ranging from ¼ to 1 inch wide, creates a durable bond between the layers.

How-to instructions begin on page 226.

# 187
## remnant redo

Take advantage of the bargain prices on upholstery piled high on fabrics store tables and turn the leftover yardage into a designer area rug. The rugged durability that makes these tapestry-type fabrics so suitable for upholstery also makes them ideal for rugs. With the right design, you can mimic the look of an expensive kilim or Oriental rug. The standard width of fabric is 54 inches, so with a 2⅔-yard remnant, you can approximate a 5×8-foot area rug. Sew a simple turned-under hem, and add heavy fringe to complete the remnant-to-rug transformation.

# fantastic floorcloths

## Quickly put your best foot forward
### with these one-of-a-kind floor coverings.

# 188
## crisp canvas

Brighten any room with a sunny floor.
Stencils and masking tape make painting
a canvas floorcloth like this a breeze.
Tape off squares for the interior pattern and
paint flowers or other designs freehand.

# 189

## savvy spots

Inspired by an Amish penny quilt, this floor covering is actually made from commercial-grade linoleum. Trace a 3×4-foot rectangle and cut along the lines with a utility knife and straightedge. Using acrylic paint, apply the background color to the linoleum. Mark and paint a 3-inch border. Trace a 6-inch round template, allowing edges of circles to touch; paint the circles. Trace 2½-inch circles in the center of the larger ones; paint in contrasting colors. After the acrylic dries, cover with a coat of varnish.

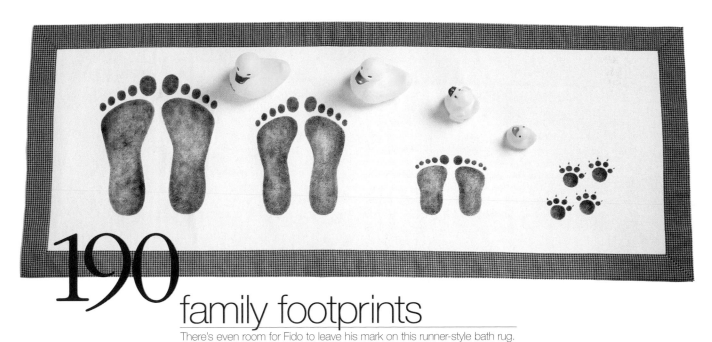

# 190

## family footprints

There's even room for Fido to leave his mark on this runner-style bath rug.
How-to instructions begin on page 226.

# painted floors

Painting yourself into a corner is unheard of
with our suggestions for **fancy footwork**.

## 191

### sweetly swedish

Instead of covering an imperfect floor with a rug or carpet, give it a fresh coat
of paint and a stenciled garland. Once-noticeable flaws will take a backseat.
To play up the crisp blue-and-white scheme in this room, we painted the floor
white, then stenciled a Swedish-inspired garland of leaves and branches. The
oval design defines the sitting space, just as an area rug would.
How-to instructions begin on page 226.

# checking in 192

Wood floors are naturally beautiful, and they become even more special when embellished with a simple design. With the wood grain still showing through its painted-on squares, the checkerboard floor *below* has European flair. The trick is to dilute oil paint with mineral spirits. If you don't want the grain to be visible, use less mineral spirits. The 23-inch squares are perfectly sized for this dining area, but you can make them larger or smaller to suit your room.

How-to instructions begin on page 226.

# wooden
# wonder

With a bit of fool-the-eye trickery, you can get the look of an old-time plank floor, *above* and *right,* without the cost. Inexpensive plywood has been aged by banging it with various hand tools. The clever plank replication comes from using a permanent marking pen to draw lines. Our cost? Just $1.40 per square foot—even less if you use an existing subfloor!

How-to instructions begin on page 226.

## 193

## 194

# paint by
# numbers

Help kids learn their numbers and ABCs by using large stencils and bright-color paint to randomly scatter numerals and letters across a playroom floor.

How-to instructions begin on page 226.

**another idea:** Cut your own stencils by using simple shapes from coloring books or purchased die-cut shapes. For older children, spell out short words on the floor. Have fun creating themed rooms. If your child loves cats, for example, stencil words such as "meow," "kitty," or "purr" across the floor.

# 195
## curlicue craze

Vinyl flooring may withstand the test of time, but its dated designs don't. With a curlicue-stamped floor, this bathroom gets a fresh new look. To start, we painted the floor white. After it dried, we stamped on the design. With the popularity of stamping as a hobby, you'll easily find a design just right for your room.

How-to instructions begin on page 226.

# 196

## tape trick

Transform the character of a boring wood floor with black electrical tape. Measure carefully and apply the tape in straight lines. Snapping plumb lines with chalk and string before starting will provide a template to trace with tape. Weave the tape lines over and under for a finished look. When you're ready for a new design, the tape pulls up easily and won't leave any marks.

# 197
## a step above

In the mood to do a little landscaping? Forget the spade, and grab a paintbrush instead. This curving front step gains curb appeal with a meandering vine design. Paint the vine as it would grow naturally—graceful, free, and uncontrolled—then give the entrance a warm welcome with a grouping of potted plants and a twig wreath.

How-to instructions begin on page 226.

## set in concrete

A back porch's drab slab becomes a lively conversation area with a punch of pattern, *left* and *above*. Use concrete stain, available in a multitude of colors at home centers and paint stores, for a whimsical flower-and-star design on your floor. The stain soaks into the porous concrete for all-weather durability. (Regular floor paint will eventually flake on moist concrete.) Paint the star "rug" in an area that will define the seating. If you don't have time for a design, a simple all-over solid-color stain will still lift concrete out of the doldrums.

How-to instructions begin on page 226.

## follow the brick road

Bricklaying may require a special skill, but not this faux-brick creation that dresses up concrete surfaces. The design, which can indicate traffic patterns or be applied across an entire floor, simply requires a few household sponges and brick-color concrete stain. Cut the sponges to the desired brick sizes, dip into the stain, blot off excess, and press onto the concrete to create "bricks." The concrete's original gray color serves as "mortar."

How-to instructions begin on page 226.

# fireplace focus

As a room's focal point, a fireplace and mantel deserve extra attention. These ideas earn glowing reviews.

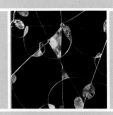   

# squared away 200

No expensive frames, no elaborate matting, no nail holes in the wall—what more could you ask for in a piece of art? Painted directly onto the wall above the mantel, the geometric painting creates a striking arrangement that is easy on the budget. Because the shapes are so simple—just squares and a circle—you can paint this masterpiece in less than a day. The design also works well for other areas that beg for attention, such as above a headboard.

How-to instructions begin on page 226.

# picture this

## 201

If your mantel lacks built-in bookshelves to display items of interest, you can still achieve a similar look. Inexpensive picture ledges like these create eye-catching space for photos, books, and other favorite objects. Install the ledges to the right and left of the mantel's center for an asymmetrical arrangement. For the look of a modern art gallery, set black-and-white photos in white mats and simple frames, and add metallic splashes with inexpensive vases or sculptures. For color and warmth, bring on the books. Prop them upright or stack them on top of one another to vary the height and look. **another idea**: For a more traditional display, use pieces of thick crown molding, available at home centers, as the ledges, and select more ornate picture frames.

## 202 dish it up

Head to the china cabinet to create an heirloom mantel display. Delicate dessert plates become works of art when hung from wire plate hangers. A pitcher doubles as a vase, and silver serving pieces add sparkle. For the most interest, mix items with different textures and place them in odd-number groupings on and above the mantel. Fresh flowers and a dainty lace doily complete the look of this easy-change still life. If you're short on china pieces, look for castaways at garage sales and antiques stores—you often can get bargain prices on incomplete sets.

## 203 screen gem

When it comes to decorating, it's all in the details. This fireplace screen gleans all the colors in the room to make an artful focal point in front of the firebox. And who would guess that the color actually is tissue paper glued onto wire loops, not costly stained glass? To start, we had an ironworks company form a 38×30-inch frame for about $50; if you have an old fireplace screen, you can remove the screen and use the existing frame to fashion your own design. *Note:* This screen is for decorative purposes only and should not be placed in front of a fire. How-to instructions begin on page 226.

## 204 we have your number

Preventing your fireplace from looking like a big black hole during the off-season is as easy as 1-2-3. When the flames flicker out, stack logs in the firebox and decorate the ends with house numbers. For the most interest, use numbers of different styles. You'll find a variety at home centers and discount stores. Look for old metal numbers at antiques stores, too. Easier yet, recycle old numbers you've thrown into a box in the garage. The more rustic and weathered, the better.

## 206
## kindling catchall

Old sap buckets are some of the most versatile containers you can have around the house. Filled with kindling, the rustic sap buckets cast a golden glow even when there isn't a fire crackling. If there are no children in the house, use a small urn to keep matches handy (remember to put them out of the reach of visiting youngsters!). Look for vintage sap buckets for $15 or less at flea markets, antiques stores, and online auction sites. Reproductions also are available at home furnishings stores for about $20. Buy different colors to change seasonally.

# 205 stamp of approval

Consider the wall space above a mantel to be a blank canvas—we sure did! This arrangement started with six blank artist's canvases, which we painted and stamped. The canvases, available at art supply stores and already stretched on a frame and primed, are ready for latex or crafts paint. We bought leaf stamps to complement the fireplace's earthy cherry woodwork and rough brick, but any stamp design will work. The large canvas, simply painted in four color blocks, anchors the arrangement and allows the blue vase with flowering branches to become part of the artwork. The three small canvases along the top act as a pattern bridge between the center canvas and the side canvases, which we stamped with an overall maple-leaf pattern. Artwork has never been so affordable!

**another idea:** Use rubber stamps to coordinate window treatments with the artwork. Stamp a complementary design on cornices (as shown here), valances, or plain sheer panels.

# stair style

Step up your stairway decorating with easy embellishments.

# 207
## letter perfect

Spell out your style with a stenciled alphabet that marches down the stairs. Thirteen steps make an ideal choice for an alphabet pattern like this one; other folk art stencil patterns are available at crafts and decorating stores.
How-to instructions begin on page 226.

## 208 brasslike tactics

Painted dowels and screw eyes take the place of expensive brass rods to hold a stair runner rug in place. For even more interest, paint the risers in colors taken from the runner.
How-to instructions begin on page 226.

## 209 up the wallpaper

Two chintz-inspired wallpapers perk up a stairway and turn it into a focal point. A black-and-white check border adds even more punch.
How-to instructions begin on page 226.

## 210 looking up

Climb your own stairway to heaven with risers sponge-painted to resemble a cloudy sky. Paint the risers and surrounding woodwork white, and then apply blue paint with a natural sea sponge.
How-to instructions begin on page 226.

## 211

## runner redux

Design a runner that shows off your beautiful hardwood floors. Painted stairs are easier to maintain because they require less vacuuming. Simply use stencils, tape, and paint to create a geometric design that runs up and down the staircase.

# 212
## center of attention

This runner couldn't be easier to care for, or to create. Paint a wide stripe along the center of the stairs with floor and deck paint. Paint stripes in the colors of your choice. Finish with a heart or other simple motif.

How-to instructions begin on page 226.

# kitchen
## accents

Your kitchen will go from
functional to sensational
with these clever concepts that organize,
utilize, and economize in style.

# 213
## gourmet storage

Create a hanging storage system that takes its cue from a pot rack hung from a ceiling. Purchase a silver-tone curtain rod. Screw two cup hooks into the bottom of an upper cabinet, thread fabric strips through the hooks, and tie the fabric to support each end of the curtain rod. Use needle-nose pliers to bend old forks into hook shapes. Bend tines in a similar manner. Place the forks over the rod; hang utensils, cooking mitts, and other lightweight items from the tines.

# 214
## make a 'splash

Install a fresh-as-a-daisy kitchen backsplash by rearranging tiles into a floral pattern. Easy-to-install mesh-back tiles are the basis for this technique. Simply pop out a few white tiles and substitute colors to form the design.

How-to instructions begin on page 226.

# 215
## my design

If you can't find tiles that match your decor or are stuck with a plain ceramic background, paint your own design. A wide array of precut stencils and several types of tile and glass paint make decorating any smooth glassy surface a snap.

# 216
## a different angle

Common plaster laths come to the forefront of the kitchen wall when applied to the surface as the backsplash. Terra-cotta counter tiles are the perfect match—both in color and texture.

How-to instructions begin on page 226.

# dig in

Give an old-fashioned kitchen a fresh bistro look by revamping plain white cabinets with stencils. Use the same fork and spoon stencil for the shadow and the main image. Lightly draw a center placement line for each stencil. Shift the stencil to the right ½ inch, and paint a thin line of medium gray for the shadow. Realign stencil to the center; fill in with color.

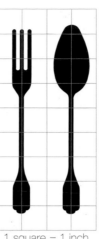

1 square = 1 inch

217

# 218
## display's the thing

Scavenge your garage or shed for a weathered item like this old iron fencing, which organizes towels and cooking utensils in a unique way. Before using salvaged pieces, seal worn paint finishes on wood and metal with a protective coat of clear water-base or oil-base polyurethane.

# 219
## clever caddy

Devise an impromptu bar by outfitting a 1940s kitchen cart with cocktail shakers, mix-and-match glassware, and bartending books. A casually propped oil painting anchors this ensemble. Look for collectibles at flea markets, antiques stores, and garage sales.

# 220
## artful arranging

Spice up a windowsill or the area behind your sink with a collection of glass bottles and jars filled with your favorite blooms or dried flowers. Arrange old Mason jars, jam jars, and water and wine bottles to create an asymmetrical display that glimmers in the sun.

# 221 | tin-stamped style

Want to update your cabinets without spending a lot of money? To re-create a vintage look like this, where kitchen cabinets resemble pie safes from yesteryear, shop flea markets or home stores for old ceiling tins.

### START TO FINISH

STEP 1. Have the ceiling tin sections cut into squares at a home center.

STEP 2. Use a miter box and a handsaw to cut quarter-round moldings into appropriate lengths to form squares for the tin sections.

STEP 3. Remove cabinet door from box; lay flat. Hold a tin square in place on the cabinet door; position a molding piece along one edge of the tin. Use an electric screwdriver to screw through the molding and tin, and into the door.

STEP 4. Using three more molding pieces, form a square around the tin square. Repeat the process until each cabinet door is decorated.

# 222
## spotlight the ceiling

Be original! Wallpaper the ceiling to jazz up your kitchen without making the space seem crowded. The simple elements of this kitchen—white cabinets, countertops, and appliances—provide a quiet backdrop for the visual activity above.

# 223
## pin it up

Put a cork in it—or at least on it. A cork backsplash adds texture—and a ready display for photos, notes, and mementos. Purchase enough 12-inch-square cork tiles to cover the backsplash area. Apply a coat of sealer to the cork before installing to make it less susceptible to water damage or food stains.

## 224

## what a dish

Look above eye level and stencil plain soffits with a dish motif. From a crafts store or home decorating center, choose a stencil pattern that fills one-half to two-thirds of the soffit depth—anything less is too small and gets lost visually. Choose light pastel colors for a bright, airy look.

## chalk it up

The chalkboard-in-a-cabinet *at left* makes prime use of a kitchen work zone to help busy families stay connected. Just paint the recessed panel of a cabinet with chalkboard paint, available at home centers and paint stores. Add a ledge to keep the chalk and eraser handy.

## flying the coop

Talk about kitchen cabinet resurfacing: No-frills chicken wire and pastoral toile fabric are the basis for the showy cabinets *at right.* The recessed cabinet panels were replaced with a soft layer of pink toile and a light-hearted layer of chicken wire for a homespun touch in a cottage-style kitchen. For a more casual and airier look, forgo the fabric and let the chicken wire fly solo.

## shelf life

No need to keep pottery treasures hidden behind cupboard doors. Fill shelves with colorful collections— or even everyday dishes—for all to enjoy. This trio of wood shelves with curving support brackets gains old-fashioned flair when backed by a wall covered with beaded board. Look for inexpensive, easy-to-install shelves in home centers. Many shelves can be painted to match your decor.

# artistic tile

Whether on a backsplash, floor,
or wall, creative use of tile and mosaic
is sure to be a focal point.

# 228

## mosaic magic

Make the shower the centerpiece of your bathroom by adding
a splash of color with a broken-tile mosaic. Scavenge home
improvement stores for broken tiles you can buy at a discount.

# 229
## hearth warming

Taupe, white, and black tiles form a graphic mosaic hearth. Large floor tiles, broken and pieced back together, create design symmetry and rhythm. The neutral colors prevent the hearth from grabbing too much attention. How-to instructions begin on page 226.

## wall nuts

A hodgepodge of tiles, flowerpots, pottery, and found objects becomes a work of art when applied to the wall above a sink. The free-flowing, rough-edged design *below* is highlighted by freehand swirls painted onto the wall. How-to instructions begin on page 226.

# 230
## that's the breaks

Don't get broken up over shattered plates—use them to make a serving tray. Damaged floral plates form a beautiful mosaic in the center. Bone buttons and a strand of pearly beads complete the graceful look. It all comes together in a purchased picture frame with handles added.

# 231

# homemade mosaic 232

Recycle bits and pieces of broken plates, cups, vases, or tiles into a stylish mosaic table like the one at *right* to enliven a sunroom, porch, or patio. Homemade tile mosaics allow you to coordinate colors and patterns to fit your decorating scheme. If you can't wait until you save enough dish shards, buy cracked or chipped pieces at a secondhand store or garage sale, and make your own fragments. Then give an old wooden end table a fresh coat of paint, and start sowing the "seeds" for a mosaic masterpiece.

How-to instructions begin on page 226.

## shell appeal

Collect too many shells on vacation? Use them to turn a boring terra-cotta pot into a from-the-sea treasure. How-to instructions begin on page 226.

233

# just add
# paint

With a can of paint and a bit of imagination, you can leave your own brush marks all about the house.

# 234 check this out

Transform furniture as your children grow. This checkerboard pattern updates a young girl's bed and armoire. To make their rooms distinctively theirs, let the kids choose the paint colors and fabrics.

# 235 spread color

Paint your own duvet cover in colors and patterns to match your room.
How-to instructions begin on page 226.

## 236

## coming up roses

Tiny lamps placed on a mantel or a side table add drama or balance to a vignette. This rosebud lamp shade shines with a free-form miniature rose design. We lightly misted the shade with water to promote extra bleeding of the paint for an ultrachalky, watercolor effect. (A fabric shade is a must; a paper or plastic shade won't absorb the water to create the same effect.) Use a permanent black marking pen to outline the buds and leaves. Don't worry if the detailing doesn't conform exactly to the shape of the painted design—coloring outside the lines is perfectly fine.
How-to instructions begin on page 226.

# back to life

Instead of carting an old chair to the trash, reupholster it with your own canvas. Let your artistic instincts take over by painting the canvas freehand or by tracing an image onto fabric using a slide projector.

before

## 237

238

## sleep ea-z-z-zy

Add your mark to plain, store-bought bedding with stencils or transfers.

How-to instructions begin on page 226.

# 239
## glassy looking

Old or reproduction perfume bottles, pill vials, and other small glass vessels are transformed into miniature works of art—perfect for tiny flower bouquets. A special glass paint is the decorating secret.
How-to instructions begin on page 226.

## 240 serve it with stencils

Next time you're at the discount store, pick up a solid-color tablecloth to make this easy project for your next picnic. Purchase stencils or make your own design, such as this watering can. Arrange stencils as desired, pin them to the tablecloth, and paint.

## 241 garden art

Frame a garden-style view with an easy etched-glass hanging. Beautiful in its simplicity, this artwork features a watering can motif made with glass-etching cream, available at crafts stores. You can easily substitute your own garden-inspired design in lieu of the watering can. How-to instructions begin on page 226.

**another idea:** To play up the theme on the glass hanging, incorporate outdoorsy items, such as old garden tools or birdhouses, throughout a room. Have fun seeking out your themed collectibles at antiques stores and garage sales.

# 242 it's a natural

Natural fibers are all the rage in decorating, and incorporating the look into your home is a breeze with an inexpensive sisal or bamboo rug. To add character to this bamboo bath mat, we stenciled from-the-forest forms and hues. And to keep the leafy design lively, position the leaf-frond stencil to face in multiple directions. The result? A natural beauty! How-to instructions begin on page 226.

## easy molding 243

You can skip using wood and a saw to add architectural detailing to your walls when you do it with stencils. Trims at the top and bottom of the walls frame the pattern in between. Check home centers and crafts stores for stencils to create a wallpaper pattern, and for a ceiling molding design and baseboard topper.

244

## bedtime story

Surrounded by a field of stenciled daisies, this headboard is painted directly onto the wall as a whimsical substitute for the real thing. Even the linens sport a few of the matching flower motifs. How-to instructions begin on page 226.

# the
# ottoman

Pull up a chair and plop your feet down—
or up, depending on the height of your
footstool. You'll be comfy enough to
make a sleeping dog jealous.

# 245

## something's afoot

Nothing accents a living room or family room like a practical footstool that can double as a convenient table beside a chair. Paint or stain unfinished furniture legs to match other furnishings.

# 246

## terrific tuffet

Add more height and cushiony comfort to a plain ottoman by stacking a pillow on top. Use decorative buttons and cord to anchor the pillow to the ottoman.

# 247
## create a cube

Foam furniture? You bet! It's light and comfortable. Start with a 20×20×20-inch foam cube stiff enough to sit on. Cover the foam block with a fitted fabric cover that has a zipper running around three sides at the top, then disguise the zipper with a fitted partial cover that slips over the cube. Line the topper with a lipped welt cord in the seam.

# 248
## dress a drawer

Transform an old drawer into a footstool with secret storage. You need only basic woodworking skills to build it.

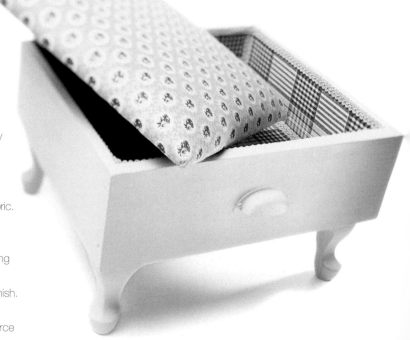

START TO FINISH

STEP 1. Prime the drawer before painting.

STEP 2. Attach four legs, which you can purchase from an upholstery supply store or home center.

STEP 3. Make the top by cutting a piece of ⅜-inch plywood slightly larger than the outside top edges of the drawer. Cut a piece of ¼-inch plywood slightly smaller than the inside of the drawer.

STEP 4. Wrap the top of the ⅜-inch piece with foam and cotton batting, stapling them to the underside of the plywood; cover with fabric.

STEP 5. Cover the ¼-inch plywood with batting and fabric in the same manner.

STEP 6. Glue together the back sides of the plywood pieces, using wood glue.

STEP 7. Add gimp around the edges of the fabric to dress up the finish.

STEP 8. Line the drawer with complementary fabric.

*NOTE:* Never sit on a stool made from a drawer unless you reinforce the bottom.

# petite **tuffets**

Little Miss Muffet had it right.

Tuffets can be a great place to **relax**.

## 249
## stylistic overtones

A gathered skirt gives a formal look to the simple lines of a bench, *above left.*

Upholstery tacks and fringe lend a traditional feel to a small footstool, *above.*

Drape fabric over a padded tuffet, then hold it in place with cording for the simplest treatment of all, *left.*

How-to instructions begin on page 226.

# divide &
## decorate

Leave your dividing dilemmas
at the door with these
posh partitions and innovative
closet door makeovers.

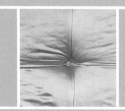  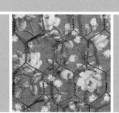 

# 250
## paper it

Who says wallpaper is just for walls? Paper lends a custom-finished look to doors and cabinets, and draws attention to a room's architectural details. When trimmed with molding, as shown here, the paper looks like a recessed panel. Choose a heavy, vinyl-coated paper for the best wearability.

# 251
## define
## intervention

Easily establish an entryway in a walk-right-in room with a folding screen. Not only does a well-coordinated screen define the entry, it also keeps coats, backpacks, and clutter neatly out of sight from the rest of the room. How-to instructions begin on page 226.

## make adjustments

Louvered panels shout Southern veranda, no matter their location. Vary the height of adjustable panels to increase visual interest, but keep the width and style the same to establish unity. How-to instructions begin on page 226.

# 252

# beautiful backdrop

Accent your bed with a screen instead of a headboard. Begin with salvaged closet doors connected by hinges, and dress them up with antique plates. Rub fresh paint lightly over the doors with steel wool for a patina effect; then coat with a tinted glaze. Painted-on ribbons appear to suspend the plates—plate hangers actually hold them in place.

253

# 251
## a trellis nature

Welcome in the great outdoors with a garden trellis
converted to window screens. Covering the lower
portion of the screens with fabric provides privacy;
leaving the top open lets the sun shine in.
How-to instructions begin on page 226.

# 255

## three-peat

Open the door to great design. In this case, make it three
doors. A trio of hollow-core doors covered with mix-and-match
wallpaper requires minimal woodworking skills to construct.
How-to instructions begin on page 226.

# 256

## from ho-hum to amazing

Be inspired by nature and turn an
ordinary door into something
extraordinary. Don't worry if your
wood cuts are flawed—that just adds
to the rustic, natural look.
How-to instructions begin on page 226.

# 257 | fenced in

Go country by coupling cheerful fabric with chicken wire on inexpensive bifolds. To create a recessed appearance (and hide the wire's stapled edges), frame each fabric-and-wire block with white-painted screen molding. Miter the corners of the screen molding; mount with finishing nails. Set the nails, fill with putty, and add a dab of paint.

# 258

## french connection

Create a French-door look for bifold closet doors with fabric and ribbon bows. Choose a fabric with a small repeat pattern—a stripe, geometric, or floral—that lends itself to a long, vertical application. Paint the doors a shade darker than the wall color and deck them with fabric panels, softly pleated into an hourglass shape. Use curtain rods that mount almost flush with the surface so doors open and close easily.

# 259

## making waves

Throw a curve into your room's decor with whimsical bifold doors that mimic ocean waves.
Blend a two-tone paint finish with the contours of decorative trim found in home supply
stores or specialty catalogs. Position the molding at least 2 inches in from the door edges.
Paint the pulls to blend with the interior panels.

## posh
## padding

Add glamour to common windows with a tufted folding screen. Choose a material that complements your decorating scheme and use it on other pieces to unify the room. This screen is padded with champagne silk. Khaki silk, repeated from the sofa, provides contrasting welting.

# 261
## take a real look-see

A basic folding screen takes on a new role when a metal window screen is stapled into the frame to diffuse the view on the lower panels. The open upper sections allow unobstructed light and breezes through.

# 262
## great suspense

Divide a room and increase its function with salvaged windows. Create the feel of an alfresco bistro by framing an intimate dining spot with stained-glass windows hung from the ceiling. Place screw eyes in the window frame to correspond with swag or plant hooks anchored in the ceiling by toggle bolts.

# kids' corner

Color is the name of the game when decorating children's rooms. Kid-friendly projects with fun fabrics and clever paint jobs are sure to delight.

# 263

## secret garden

Who would have thought that a trip to a home center could yield such fabulous finds for a girl's bedroom? Picket fencing and lattice painted white inspire a fantasy garden in this room. Below the window, the fencing is attached directly to the wall to create a gentle boundary between indoors and out. A floor-to-ceiling piece of lattice nailed to the wall acts as a trellis, and wooden planters placed along the floor bloom with a mix of real and wooden flowers. Easy to find and cut, these items can be used solo or in concert and are easily adapted to any room. **another idea:** Mount planters at windowsill level, attach short pieces of picket fencing as a valance or cornice, and use a real trellis rather than lattice. For extra impact, stencil flowers or leaves on the fencing or lattice.

# 264

## on display

Kids love pinning up their treasures, but unadorned cork bulletin boards plainly can be boring. Covered in a colorful checked fabric and framed with rickrack, though, a bulletin board goes beyond mere function to become a part of the room's decor. Dig through your fabric scraps or buy an inexpensive remnant. Cut the fabric slightly larger than the board; then wrap it around the board, stapling the cut edges to the back. Hot-glue rickrack, cording, or ribbon along the edges for a finished look. Below the board, use pegs on a rack to pick up the colors of the checked fabric and serve as handy display hangers.

# 265

## baby steps

Goodbye, fussy fabric and ornate hardware. Hello, old bedspread and blue tennies. This clever window treatment speaks to the nursery: The nubby curtain, cut from a chenille bedspread, adds cuddly warmth, and the baby-shoe tiebacks are oh-so-cute. **another idea:** Look for window-treatment inspiration in unexpected places. Pink ballerina slippers, ice skates, or even rubber flippers can all stand in as kid-friendly tiebacks. For curtains, consider using a fleece stadium blanket, flannel sheets, or beach towel. If necessary, you can sew towels together to achieve the desired size.

# 266

## a storybook ending

To put the finishing touches on a child's room, use a favorite storybook as artwork. Flea markets and garage sales are great places to find colorful books that are cheap enough to make ripping them apart painless. We found an oversize book for just $5, then had this page professionally matted and framed for about $40.

# 267

## under construction

Instead of splurging on costly children's furniture, create a fun-loving construction zone perfect for little operators, *opposite*. Use 2×4-inch studs for the framework shelving unit. Vary the heights of the shelves to accommodate your tyke's favorite toys. A barricade rail fabricated from painted 1×4s stands in as a clever chair rail, and a sawhorse desk offers space for getting down to business.

# 268

## lovely lullaby

Cover a wicker basket with gingham and fit it with foam for a country-style baby carrier. How-to instructions begin on page 226.

## hide and seek

Teach an old dresser new tricks by transforming its drawers into under-the-bed storage bins. Starting with a $50 thrift-shop dresser, we traded the outdated hardware and a dark-stained finish for a few coats of cottage-white paint and new glass handles. Four casters screwed into the corners make it easy for kids to roll the drawers in and out from under the bed. Filled with clothes or toys, the freewheeling catchall is a handy helper.

# 270
## under the big top

Bring a circus of delight to your baby's room by turning a simple wardrobe into a storage and display unit fit for Barnum and Bailey. To make the tepee-style cornice and panels, select a bright-colored fabric that coordinates with the bedding. Paint the walls a subdued shade to avoid a look that's too busy.

300 Decorating Ideas Under $100

273

272

## 271 top it off

Put fabric scraps to good use by fashioning a tab-top valance, *above left and opposite.* Cheery yellow chenille gives a cozy touch up high. Tabs and banding sewn from different fabrics add homespun charm. Because the patterns and colors aren't too cutesy, the valance offers plenty of decorating possibilities down the road.

How-to instructions begin on page 226.

## 272 please be seated

Studded with glass finials, this whimsical chair is worthy of a little prince or princess. First, give an old wooden chair a fresh coat of paint to complement your child's bedroom or playroom. Then drill two small holes onto the top of the chair back in a place where the finials can be screwed in securely. Look for finials in a wide variety of shapes and styles in the curtain hardware section of discount stores and home centers. **another idea:** To jazz up the chair even more, paint on a design that mimics the shape of the finials. Diamonds, curlicues, or other simple shapes are easy to master regardless of your artistic skills. Use stencils for more intricate designs.

## 273 sentimental favorite

Instead of keeping dear-to-the-heart items hidden in boxes in the attic, look for innovative ways to showcase them. Vintage doll clothes, *above* and *opposite,* dangle from a ribbon clothesline. If you're worried about little hands marring precious commodities, hang them out of harm's way, as was done with this clothesline that swags above French doors. Family treasures are an ideal way to add style—and emotion—to any room. **another idea:** Use ribbon or a peg rack to hang toys or photos above a changing table to keep your baby occupied.

# 274 take cover

Need a quick storage solution for your son's room? Slipcover an old table or wooden box and embellish it with coordinating trims, buttons, and piping to add a dash of splash. The finished project is perfect for stowing books and toys out of sight.

# 275

## pocket pals

A wall hanging with storage pockets is a great space saver that's easy for little ones to reach. Shape the pockets to fit specific items. Buttoned pockets keep scissors and glue out of the hands of wee ones. For bulky items, such as books, add stability by putting cardboard in the bottom of the pocket. Hang the grommeted fabric on the wall with inexpensive coat hooks.

# 276

## study hall

Inspire creative thinking with an upholstered desk. That's right—fabric can soften even a large wooden object, such as a desk or table. Use the same fabric as your window treatments or bedspread, or bring in an entirely new pattern for fun. If you're new at upholstering, choose a fabric with an allover print (solids tend to show flaws), and, budget permitting, purchase an unassembled desk so you can add the fabric before you put the pieces together. Straight-line parts are easiest to work with. You also can give a tired, timeworn piece new life by covering it with a snappy fabric. When it's time to update the room or you tire of the look, just tear off the old fabric and start anew.

How-to instructions begin on page 226.

# bath
# splash

Soak up style with these inventive ideas that add charm and function to baths big and small.

# 277
## ship ahoy

Add architectural interest to a bath by crowning a window with a colorful cornice that plays up the room's theme. A clever paint scheme gives the plain wood cornice its shipshape design. Begin with a white base coat. When it's dry, use masking tape to create the diagonal grid on the surface. Brush on a bold periwinkle paint to further the nautical theme, and remove the tape. Finish with a green border. To give the window a greater sense of height, the top of the cornice hangs 16 inches above the window.

## 278

## trendy transfers

Can't seem to find just the right shower curtain? Create your own! For a trendy look, transfer images onto a plain shower curtain. This curtain flaunts pictures of chairs from a furniture catalog. How-to instructions begin on page 226.

# 280
## personally yours

Monograms are all the rage, and *below* is an inexpensive way to incorporate them into your decor: Personalize a store-bought canvas shower curtain. Apply your monogram using fabric paint and stencils made from computer-generated letters.

# 279

## fit for a queen

Turn an everyday tub into a bathing beauty with an elegant tent of fabric draped over brackets projecting from the wall. Opt for inexpensive fabric that coordinates with your color scheme and will soothe and comfort you.

## curtain call

Don't sew? No problem! A twin-size matelassé bed coverlet hung from a tension rod with curtain ring clips becomes a stylish shower curtain. It's an easy way to coordinate a bedroom and bathroom. The reversible geometric pattern ensures that the view from inside the tub is pleasing; just use a clear plastic liner to keep the fabric dry. Almost any lightweight coverlet, blanket, or sheet can double as a shower curtain. Remember to measure the tub opening before buying the bedcover to make sure the dimensions are compatible.

281

282

## double vision

Sure, you can splurge on an expensive mirror to become a focal point above the sink. But why bother when salvaged windowpanes are just as—or even more—interesting? Two window frames outfitted with mirrors look right at home in this cottage-style bath. Forget the scraping, priming, and painting. The more weathered and rustic, the more appealing.

283

## bar none

Every bath needs room to hang towels, but the solution doesn't have to be a nondescript metal bar that steals limited wall space. Coat hooks mounted on lumber are more than just functional; they also bring a homey touch to a utilitarian space. These handy hooks once were attached to a long piece of lumber, which had been wallpapered quite a while ago. The board was cut into smaller rectangles to hang on a mere sliver of wall area. If you can't find something comparable at an antiques store, simply start from scraps of lumber. Embellish cut pieces with wallpaper to match your decor, or by stenciling or painting.

# custom cabinetry

A dated base cabinet can be the bane of a bath's existence. With an easy remake, though, this once-tired vanity now is a smart focal point. After the cabinet doors came off, the unit received a fresh coat of paint and new glass knobs. A curtain sewn from flannel sheets forms a soft replacement for the doors. Vintage accessories, including swimming pool baskets and mirrors with white-painted frames, add charm and function. How-to instructions begin on page 226.

**another idea:** Use sheeting scraps to dress up plain towels, or buy extra sheets to make a window treatment or shower curtain.

# 285
## savvy sink

One glimpse of this sink and you'll never look at enamelware the same way. With a hole drilled in its base, a floral-painted piece became a lovely sink that now bowls over guests. Purchase standard drain fittings at a home center or hardware store to complete the project.
How-to instructions begin on page 226.

# 286
## earning their stripes

Give plain-Jane towels a designer look by adding washable accents. We cut varying widths of ribbon and sewed strips together to create the multicolor stripes on the towels at *left*. You may even have odds and ends of ribbon on hand to make the trim.
How-to instructions begin on page 226.

**another idea:** Adapt this concept to embellish washcloths, shower curtains, and window treatments.

# 287
## skirt the issue

A no-fuss gathered sink skirt becomes a cute cover-up for unsightly sink plumbing. It's also an efficient way to extend storage space. Hook-and-loop fastening tape affixes the floral skirt to the sink; a finished band allows the skirt to be mounted on the front edge of the sink or under the lip, depending on which side of the band the tape is sewn on.
How-to instructions begin on page 226.

# sweet ideas

This monochromatic bath exudes an air of luxurious elegance, the result of a juxtaposition of objects, old and new. A vintage enameled medical cart is a rolling paradise of perfumes, soaps, and potpourri. Silver serving trays and clear glass cookie, candy, and apothecary jars—available at discount stores for under $20—hold little luxuries. Above the tub, wiry crates offer artful storage. Chrome hooks placed over the shower door offer a handy spot for hanging towels or robes. The clever touches add both beauty and function.

288

# outdoor
# lighting

Make your next outdoor gathering
the talk of the town with illuminating
candle displays.

   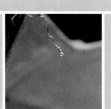

# 289
## table-side tapers

Enhance your outdoor entertaining with the glow of candles by plunging skinny tapers into sand-filled pots. Bamboo mats underneath add a decorative touch and catch dripping wax.

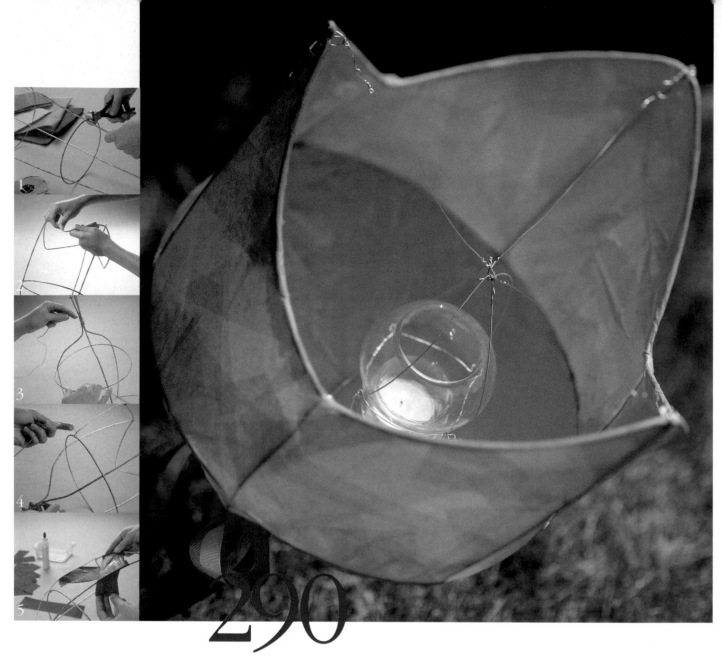

## 290

# lovely lanterns

Turn tomato cages into these scene-stealing tulip-shape lanterns.

### MATERIALS

Tomato cages
Colored tissue
  paper
Grosgrain ribbon
Thin-gauge wire
Crafts glue
Clear polyurethane spray
Wire cutters
Shallow pan
Glass lantern and votive
  candle; or a battery-
  operated lantern, glow
  stick, or flashlight

START TO FINISH

STEP 1. Using wire cutters, remove the bottom ring from the tomato cage (*photo 1*). Bend top ring of cage into a tulip-petal shape (*photo 2*). Bend the wire below the second ring to form the tulip base. Secure the base and stem with thin-gauge wire (*photo 3*).

STEP 2. To define the tulip shape and add structure to support the tissue paper, string thin-gauge wire from the bottom of V shapes, and secure it at the tulip base (*photo 4*).

STEP 3. Mix 1 part crafts glue with 1 part water in a shallow pan. Tear the tissue paper into 1½×6-inch strips. Working with one piece at a time, draw strips through the glue mixture, dragging them along the side of the pan to remove excess glue.

STEP 4. Attach the strips to the tulip frame (*photo 5*). Cover the tulip frame with three layers of tissue paper, placing it on the inside and outside of the frame. Cover the stem with green tissue paper strips. Let dry. Spray with clear polyurethane.

STEP 5. To finish, wire a glass lantern with a votive candle or a battery-operated lantern to the interior of the tulip, or use a glow stick or flashlight. Tie several colors of grosgrain ribbon into a bow at the tulip base. Hang the lantern from wire or fishing line, or stick it into the ground.

*TIP:* Work outside when making these lanterns. Stick the tulip stems into the ground; then add the messy tissue-paper strips to the frames and let dry. To preserve the lanterns, bring them indoors when it rains.

# 291
## night lights

Votive candles in jelly jars will re-create the effect of fireflies in the air. Hang the luminarias from tree branches near a dining spot to generate a chandelier effect. No need to worry about the breeze because the flames are protected.

# 292
## ground glow

Votive candles scattered among white landscaping rock illuminate a garden walkway. If the candles are on a flameproof surface, such as a concrete patio, you won't even need candleholders. In other spots, carved-stone holders like these work well.

# outdoor projects

Extend your living space by moving outdoors and decorating your patio and garden with comfortable, functional furniture and colorful accessories.

# 293

## classic comfort

Classic Adirondack furniture never goes out of style, and with good reason—it's attractive, restful, and easy to care for. A footstool invites relaxing. The curved edge of the table skirt echoes the curves of the chair back.

# 294
## covert cover-up

Have something to hide in your yard? A hinged, rough-cut folding screen that doubles as a plant stand stores easily when not in use.

How-to instructions begin on page 226.

## upward bound

Spread color on bland backdrops by growing climbers on poles. The wire grid background is practically invisible yet provides the structure many climbers need to reach new heights.

How-to instructions begin on page 226.

# 296
## rock on

Whether you share the space with someone special or stretch out with a good book, you'll want to stay all day in this double-wide Adirondack rocker.

How-to instructions begin on page 226.

# 297
## mileage marker

Set the scene for a backyard getaway with a mileage marker—planted among the shrubs—pointing to favorite destinations from the past and dream vacations to come.

# 298
## sculpture made simple

Make this ancient-looking garden sculpture with traditional papier-mâché techniques.

**START TO FINISH**

**STEP 1**. Choose a design and create an armature (the basic framework of a sculpture). Balloons work as a framework for creating heads, suns, or any spherical shape. For other shapes, try using chicken wire, which molds easily. For a smooth surface, cover a rough armature with sheets of paper and masking tape.

**STEP 2**. Shred newspaper, junk mail, and other paper scraps.

**STEP 3**. Soak the shredded paper in water until thoroughly wet; then strain excess water.

**STEP 4**. Add cellulose paste.

**STEP 5**. Blend the paper-paste mixture together with a blender or food processor. Play with the cellulose-paper proportions until a thick liquid paste forms.

**STEP 6**. Generously hand-mold the mixture onto the armature. Create different shapes and dimensions by allowing the papier-mâché to dry and sculpting new layers over it.

**STEP 7**. Once the sculpture dries, waterproof it with linseed oil, a waterproofing preparation, or butcher's wax. *Note*: You'll need to waterproof again each season.

**STEP 8**. Add pizzazz with a coat of colorful plastic dip, which comes in various colors and is available at any hardware store.

*299*

## for the birds

Thrill your backyard buddies with a sphere rolled in melted lard or peanut butter and their favorite seed. Then place in an urn within view from a window, and watch the show begin.

How-to instructions begin on page 226.

# 300
## out of sight!

Create privacy or wall off an unsightly view with a trio of trellises. Place them at angles—like half-open shutters—or line them up side by side for ultimate solitude.

How-to instructions begin on page 226.

# do it
# yourself

Like what you see?
Create your own versions of these
projects to enjoy at home.

# wall displays

## 7 Order in the House

### MATERIALS

- Old frames of similar sizes in a variety of shapes
- White mat boards
- White spray paint
- Vintage photographs
- Butcher or kraft paper
- Low-tack painter's tape
- Picture hangers and nails

### START TO FINISH

STEP 1. Trace each frame onto butcher or kraft paper and cut out the shape. Set the patterns aside.

STEP 2. Paint the frames white; let dry. Place the photographs in the frames, using white mats where needed.

STEP 3. To determine a pleasing arrangement, lay out the patterns on the floor. Align the bottom edges of some frames with the top edges of others; align some left- or right-hand edges; and center some frames over others. This will make the arrangement more cohesive.

STEP 4. When you are pleased with the arrangement, transfer the patterns to the wall and tape them in place. Check the arrangement for balance one last time. Hammer nails into the wall where needed, then replace each pattern with the corresponding frame.

## 8 Words of Wisdom

### MATERIALS

- Black pen or computer
- White paper
- Three identical black narrow-edge frames
- White mat boards

### START TO FINISH

STEP 1. Hand-letter or print out favored quotations. Use the same typeface and type size; the lengths of the quotes can be different.

STEP 2. Have a mat cut to fit each quotation or cut mat yourself. Place each mat and quotation in a frame, then hang the frames in a vertical arrangement with little space between frames.

## 9 Knock, Knock

### MATERIALS

- Old door hardware such as knobs, keys, knockers, and door plates
- Old frames to fit the hardware
- Foam-core board cut to fit the frames
- Decorative papers
- Sandpaper (optional)
- Spray adhesive
- Heavy-duty adhesive for metal
- Crafts knife
- Sawtooth hangers

### START TO FINISH

STEP 1. Arrange the hardware in the empty frames. If necessary, paint, sand, or otherwise finish each frame so it blends with the hardware. Note which hardware goes in which frame, then remove the hardware.

STEP 2. Attach a sawtooth hanger to the back of each frame.

STEP 3. Match the decorative papers to the hardware. If the paper pattern is too strong, sand it lightly to give it an aged look. Trim the paper to fit the foam-core board and affix it to the board with spray adhesive. Place the foam-core board in the frame.

STEP 4. Glue the keys, door plates, and any other flat pieces to the foam-core board. For doorknobs and other pieces with shanks, cut a small hole in the foam-core board and slide the shank through the hole. Glue the foam-core board in place.

## 10 Take a Tint

### MATERIALS

- Black-and-white or color photos with a similar theme and scale
- Frames in identical size and color
- Purchased or self-cut mat boards
- Fabric scraps for covering mat boards— small prints in subtle colors work best
- Fabric glue

# wall displays

- Foam brush
- Drapery rod
- Screw eyes
- Ribbon for hanging the pictures

## START TO FINISH

STEP 1. Locate a photo-processing store that uses a direct print-to-print machine. You may have to go to a professional photo processor instead of a local discount processor.

STEP 2. If any of the photographs are color, have black-and-white prints made from the negatives. Once all the photographs are black-and-white, have the processor make duplicates, adjusting the color controls to create the desired tint. The photos also can be enlarged, reduced, or cropped to coordinate.

STEP 3. Cut fabric 2 inches larger than the mat board on all sides, positioning the fabric to make the most of the design. Spread fabric glue over the front of the mat board and smooth the fabric in place. Wrap the margin to the back, mitering the corners, and glue it in place. Trim the fabric if necessary. To create the center opening, make an X from corner to corner. Fold the triangles to the back, trim the excess fabric, and glue the fabric to the back.

STEP 4. After the glue dries, place the photos and mats in frames. Hang a drapery rod on the wall where the pictures will be displayed. Place a screw eye on each side of the frame back near the top. Wrap ribbon through each screw eye and tie it around the drapery rod. Be sure to hang the photographs at slightly different heights.

## 12 In-Depth Analysis

### MATERIALS

- Vintage items such as photographs, keys, jewelry, and watches
- Purchased or handmade frames
- Paint for the display background
- Small nails
- Wood filler
- Archival-quality double-backed removable mounting tape

### START TO FINISH

STEP 1. Arrange the vintage items in a pleasing display, then measure to determine the size frames needed. Hold the frames to the wall and trace along the inside edges. Paint ¼ inch beyond these lines to created the colored background. Nail the frames to the wall over the painted area. Fill the nail holes.

STEP 2. Place the display items in the frames. Use small nails to hang keys, jewelry, and other objects. For photographs, use archival-quality double-backed removable mounting tape.

## 13 Shadow Play

### MATERIALS

- Birch scraps
- Saw
- Clamps (optional)
- Wood glue
- Nails
- Paint for the wall background
- Wood filler and sandpaper
- Sawtooth hanger
- Display piece (we used flowers)

### START TO FINISH

STEP 1. Cut two pieces of birch long and wide enough to hold your display. The ones shown are ½ inch thick for the shelf and ¾ inch thick for the wall support. Join them in a butt joint with the backs aligned. Secure them with glue and nails. Fill nail holes and sand the shelf smooth.

STEP 2. Make a frame from birch boards, mitering joints. Make sure frame is large enough to accommodate both the shelf and the display. Fill nail holes and sand frame. Attach sawtooth hanger to the back along the upper edge.

STEP 3. Hold the frame to the wall and trace along inside edges. Paint the wall a contrasting color, extending the paint ¼ inch beyond the marked lines. Hang frame over painted area. Nail shelf into place and add your display.

# a chair affair

### 16 Cheer for a Tie

MATERIALS

- 54-inch-wide medium-weight fabric (the amount will vary with the size of your chair)
- 5½ yards of ⅝-inch-wide grosgrain ribbon (may be different colors)

START TO FINISH

STEP 1. To determine the length of the main panel, start at the back of the chair and measure from the floor, over the back, across the seat, to the floor. Add 4 inches for hems.
STEP 2. For the width of the main panel, measure the width of the chair seat and add 8 inches for hems. Cut out the main panel.
STEP 3. For the length of the side panel, start at one side and measure from floor, across the seat, to floor. Add 4 inches for hems. For the width, measure the depth of the chair seat and add 8 inches. Cut out the side panel.
STEP 4. Press under 4 inches on the long sides of each panel, and pin in place. On the ends of each piece, turn under 1 inch twice and pin.
STEP 5. Center the side panel over the chair seat. Place the main panel over the chair. Pin the side and main panels together along the chair edges. Check the hem lengths and make any needed adjustments.
STEP 6. Topstitch the side panels to the main panel. Topstitch hems. Place the cover over the chair. Cut the ribbon into eight pairs of 12-inch-long ties. Tack the ties into place and tie the cover to the chair.

### 18 Sew What?

MATERIALS

- Approximately ⅔ yard lightweight fabric
- Water-erasable fabric marker
- Fusing tape or sewing thread
- Ribbon, twine, or string for corner ties

START TO FINISH

STEP 1. Drape the fabric over the chair seat, letting it fall past the apron (the front and side pieces under the seat and above the legs). Draw the desired hemline and mark any areas that will need to be notched out to accommodate the chair back and legs.
STEP 2. Remove fabric from the chair and even out the lines. Cut the skirt 1 inch larger all around than the marked lines. Hem all edges with topstitching or fusing tape.
STEP 3. Place the cover back on the chair. Tack ribbon, twine, or string to the four corners and tie bows to draw in the excess fabric. Use the back ties to anchor the cover to the chair.

### 19 A Star in Stripes

MATERIALS

- Medium-weight fabric (the amount will vary with the chair size)
- Water-erasable fabric marker
- Hook-and-loop tape
- Fabric glue

START TO FINISH

STEP 1. To determine the length of the main panel, start at the rear of the chair and measure the length from the floor over the top, down to the seat, across the seat, and back to the floor. Add 1½ inches for hems. For the width of the main panel, measure the space between uprights and add 1 inch.
STEP 2. For the length of the removable side panel, start at one side and measure from the floor to the seat, across the seat, and back to the floor. Add 1½ inches for hems. For the width, measure the distance between the legs and add 1 inch.
STEP 3. Cut out the two panels. Hem all edges. Cut four 17x2½-inch strips for ties. Fold each tie in half lengthwise and sew along the raw edges, leaving an opening for turning. Turn and slip-stitch the opening closed.
STEP 4. Place the main panel over the chair. Mark the placement for the ties at the seat joint. Tack the ties in place. Slide the side panel under the main panel, centering it on the chair. Glue the soft loop side of hook-and-loop tape to the underside of the main panel where the two panels overlap. Glue the rigid hook side of the tape to the corresponding spots on the side panel.

# a chair affair

## 20 Rounding Things Out

### MATERIALS
- Medium-weight fabric (the amount will vary with the chair size)
- Water-erasable fabric marker
- Kraft paper for pattern

### START TO FINISH

STEP 1. For the length of the main panel, start at the rear of the chair and measure from the seat, over the top, down to the seat, and across the seat to the front edge. Add 20 inches. For the width, use the seat width plus 2 inches.

STEP 2. For the side panels, cut two pieces of fabric 11 inches long by the depth of the seat plus hem allowances. Cut one main panel and two side panels. Hem short ends of side panels.

STEP 3. Make a paper pattern for the front and sides, dividing the panel width into three scallops. Turn up a 5-inch hem on each end of the main panel, right sides facing. Transfer the curved line to the bottom of the hems and sew along the lines. Clip the curves and trim the seam allowances. Turn the hems to the back side and press. Make the hemline for the side panels in the same manner.

STEP 4. Place the main panel over the chair and pin in place. Lay one side panel across the seat, right side down. Align one long edge with the side of the seat cover and pin in place. Repeat for the other side panel. Sew the panels to the cover.

STEP 5. To form the upper curve of the cover, place the cover on the chair, wrong side out. Carefully mark the curve of the upper edge of the chair. Sew ½ inch outside the line through both layers of fabric. Turn the cover to the right side and try it on the chair. If the fit is correct, trim away the excess fabric.

STEP 6. Hem the long edges of the cover, encasing the raw edges. Place the cover over the chair and mark the placement for the ribbon ties. Tack the ribbons in place and tie the cover to the chair.

## 21 Display a Soft Side

### MATERIALS
- Medium-weight sheer fabric (the amount will vary with the chair size)
- Water-erasable fabric marker
- Grommets and grommet tool
- 2-inch-wide sheer ribbon

### START TO FINISH

STEP 1. For the length of the main panel, start at the rear of the chair and measure from the seat, over the top, down to the seat, and across the seat to the front edge. Add 20 inches. For the width, use the seat width plus 2 inches.

STEP 2. For the side panels, cut two pieces measuring 11 inches by the depth of the seat and hem allowances. Cut one main panel and two side panels. Hem short ends of the side panels.

STEP 3. Place the main panel over the chair and pin in place. Lay one side panel across the seat, right side down, aligning its top edge with the side of the seat cover. Pin in place. Repeat for the other side panel. Sew the side panels to the cover.

STEP 4. Hem the long edges of the chair-back cover, encasing the raw edges. On all four sides of the cover, turn up the hem (about 5 inches depending on your chair) and topstitch in place, encasing the raw edges.

STEP 5. Place the cover over the chair and mark the placement for the grommets. Install the grommets according to the manufacturer's directions. Tie ribbons through the grommets to hold the cover in place.

## 23 The Great Cover-Up

### MATERIALS
- Polyester quilt batting
- Fabric for the cover
- Fabric glue
- 4¼ yards cording or ribbon for ties
- Hook-and-loop tape

### START TO FINISH

STEP 1. Cut batting to fit around the top of the chair back, covering the front, back, and upper edge. Cut fabric twice the length and twice the width of the batting. Center the batting on the fabric. Tack it in place with small dots of fabric glue. Fold the top and bottom edges of the fabric to the center of the batting and glue or slip-stitch in place. Fold the remaining two edges in to the center and glue or slip-stitch in place.

STEP 2. Fold the chair cover over the chair back. Tack 16-inch-long ties to each corner and tie the cover in place.

STEP 3. Cut two strips of batting for the seat, one to go lengthwise and one to go crosswise. Let the batting drape 6 to 8 inches over the edges. Cover each batting strip in the same manner the chair-back batting was covered.

STEP 4. Place one panel to drape over the sides of the seat. Place the other panel over it, centering both pieces. Glue the soft loop side of hook-and-loop tape to the underside of the top

# a chair affair

panel along the outer edges. Glue the rigid loop side of the hook-and-loop tape to the side panel in the corresponding spots.

STEP 5. Tack 16-inch ties to the back corners and tie the seat cover to the chair.

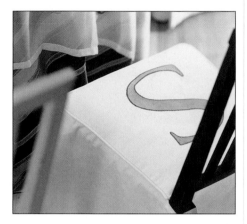

## 24 Letter Perfect

### MATERIALS

- 54-inch-wide fabric (about 3 yards, but the amount will vary with chair size)
- Kraft paper for pattern
- Contrasting nonwoven (nonfraying) fabric, such as imitation suede, for the monogram
- Paper-backed fusible webbing
- Computer-generated letter or stencil for monogram (the one shown is 10x7 inches)
- 2 yards ¼-inch-diameter piping or cording

### START TO FINISH

STEP 1. Measure the chair according to the diagram *above right*. For the skirt width, double the seat depth and add the seat-front width, plus 36 inches for box pleats, back closure, and hems. For the skirt length, measure the seat height, and add 2½ inches for seam allowances and hem. Cut out the skirt piece.

STEP 2. Trace the seat shape onto paper. Add ½-inch seam allowances around the side and front edges. Extend the seat shape to the back to create a flap that will hang to the floor with a 2-inch hem. Make small notches in this piece to fit around the structure of the chair. See the Fabric Cutting Diagram *right*. Cut out the paper pattern and try it on the chair. Make any adjustments, then cut the fabric from the pattern and hem the bottom of the flap.

STEP 3. Fuse the paper-backed fusible webbing to the contrasting monogram fabric. Trace the letter onto fabric and cut out. Peel off the backing and center the letter on the seat fabric. Fuse it in place according to the manufacturer's directions. If desired, sew around the appliqué with a narrow, tight zigzag (satin stitch).

STEP 4. Using handmade or purchased piping, sew piping to the seat-piece front and sides along the seam line.

STEP 5. Hem one long edge and both short edges of the skirt. Pin the center of the skirt to the center front of the seat piece with right sides facing and raw edges aligned. Pin out toward the corners. At each corner, fold back 3 inches of skirt fabric then fold the fabric forward again. Repeat in the opposite direction to make box pleats as shown *below right*. Continue pinning the skirt around the seat. Sew the skirt to the seat piece. Clip the fabric seams.

STEP 6. Cut four 12x1-inch ties. Hem the short edges. Turn the long edges under ¼ inch, then fold the ties in half lengthwise, encasing the raw edges. Topstitch along both edges. Tack one end of one tie to the top of the skirt back and a second tie to the center of the skirt back. Repeat for the other end of the skirt back.

STEP 7. Place the cover over the chair and tie the ties. Flip the back flap over the back of the skirt.

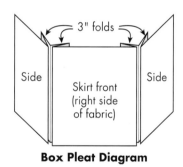

**Measuring Chair Diagram**

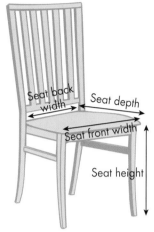

**Box Pleat Diagram**

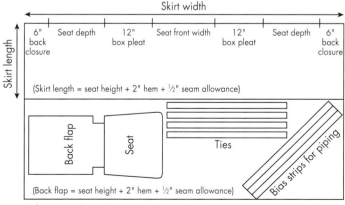

**Fabric Cutting Diagram**

# in a new light

## 25 Crystal Clear

### MATERIALS

- Colored lamp shade
- Lacy art paper
- Spray adhesive
- Sewing needle
- Chandelier crystals

### START TO FINISH

STEP 1. Lay the lamp shade on its side atop a piece of lacy art paper. Gently roll the shade over the art paper, tracing along the top and bottom edges with a pencil as it rolls. Cut out the art-paper pattern with scissors, adding ¼ inch to each edge.

STEP 2. Test the fit of the art-paper pattern on the lamp shade; cut the ends so they will overlap on the shade ½ inch. Spray the wrong side of the art paper with spray adhesive. Wrap the art paper around the lamp shade and smooth out, overlapping the ends and folding the top and bottom edges to the inside.

STEP 3. Use a needle to pierce small, evenly spaced holes through the lamp shade along the bottom edge. Insert chandelier crystals through the holes.

## 26 Uplifting Effect

### MATERIALS

- Plain white chandelier shades
- Assorted ribbon, fabric, and upholstery trims
- Stickers, pre-inked stamps, and other paper crafts supplies
- Acrylic paint
- Low-tack painter's tape
- Hot-glue gun and glue sticks
- Tacky glue

### START TO FINISH

#### PATCHWORK SHADE (1)

Cut 1-inch squares of assorted calico fabrics. Brush the backs of the squares with tacky glue and place them on the shade. Glue narrow strips of rickrack around the edges of each square.

#### BALL-FRINGE SHADE (2)

Hot-glue ball fringe or other trim to the lower edge of the shade, turning under the raw edge.

#### RIBBON-TRIMMED SHADE (3)

Cut patterned grosgrain ribbon to fit the top and bottom edges of the shade, adding ½ inch for turning under. Hot-glue the ribbon to the shade, turning under the raw edges.

#### STRIPED SHADE (4)

Mask off stripes with low-tack painter's tape. Seal the tape to the shade with a rigid plastic card, such as a credit card. Paint the exposed areas with two or more coats of acrylic paint. When the paint dries, remove the tape. Because the shade is wider at the bottom, painted stripes will also be wider at the bottom.

#### SPIRAL-RIBBON SHADE (5)

Glue a strip of ⅝-inch-wide grosgrain ribbon to the shade in a spiral pattern. Tuck the ends to the inside at the top and bottom. Add rows of ribbon parallel to the first row.

#### GEOMETRIC SHADE (6)

Scatter small geometric stickers over the shade, sealing the edges with a rigid plastic card. Paint the shade with two or more coats of acrylic paint. When paint dries, carefully remove stickers.

#### POLKA-DOT SHADE (7)

Apply clusters of pre-inked round mini stamps to a matte-finish shade; ink will not dry on a gloss-finish lamp shade.

# in a new light

## 28 Added Texture
### MATERIALS
- Plaster candlestick-style lamp
- Pastel, silver, and pearlescent spray paints
- Tiny seashells
- Tacky crafts glue
- Foam paintbrush
- Spray sealer
- Linen-texture lamp shade
- Starfish
- Hot-glue gun and glue sticks

### START TO FINISH
STEP 1. Spray-paint the lamp base with pastel paint. Highlight with a mist of silver and pearlescent spray paints.
STEP 2. Lay the lamp horizontally. Brush a thick coat of tacky glue onto the neck of the lamp. Press seashells into the glue, packing them tightly. After the glue dries, turn the lamp, and glue shells to the next section. Continue until the entire neck is coated with shells. Spray the base with sealer.
STEP 3. Hot-glue small starfish to the shade. Mist the embellished shade with silver and pearlescent paints.

## Corded Shade
### MATERIALS
- Plaster lamp with a paper shade
- Acrylic paints in light green and dark green
- Foam paintbrushes
- Clean, lint-free paint rags
- Glue-on studs
- Narrow cording
- Tacky crafts glue or epoxy

### START TO FINISH
STEP 1. Paint the lamp base light green; let dry. Rag on the dark green, letting some of the light green show through for an aged look. Rub a small amount of paint on the shade.
STEP 2. Measure the shade top and divide it evenly into increments. Divide the shade bottom into twice as many increments. Cut the cording into pieces slightly longer than the height of the shade. Glue one end of each cord to the marks at the top of the shade; glue the free ends to every other spot along the bottom edge of the shade. Glue a stud over each mark.

## 30 Lasting Impressions
### MATERIALS
- Acrylic crafts paints in periwinkle, rose, yellow, and green
- Small containers
- Plain white fabric lamp shade
- #6 flat paintbrush
- 1-inch paintbrush (optional)
- Spray water bottle

### START TO FINISH
STEP 1. For each paint, mix equal parts paint and water in a small container.
STEP 2. Use the flat paintbrush to randomly paint periwinkle, rose, and yellow roses and green leaves on the lamp shade. For roses, use a squiggly, spiral motion that starts in the center of the flower; let the lines bleed together. If desired, use the 1-inch paintbrush for smaller areas.
STEP 3. To promote more bleeding of the colors, lightly mist the shade with water. Let dry.

## 34 Timely Statement
### MATERIALS
- Matte-finish paper shade
- Acrylic paint
- Foam paintbrush
- Clip-art images
- Decoupage medium

### START TO FINISH
STEP 1. Paint the shade with two coats of acrylic paint. After the paint dries, place the shade on a lighted lamp and check for streaks or thin spots. Touch up the paint until the color is even. (Do not use a gloss-finish shade. The paint will peel away from a shiny surface.)
STEP 2. Photocopy the clip-art images, then cut them out. Coat the backs of the cutouts with decoupage medium, and smooth the images onto the lamp shade, as *below*. Finish the lamp shade with two or more coats of decoupage medium.

# in a new light

## 36 Natural Shade

### MATERIALS
- Matte-finish paper shade
- Wide low-tack painter's tape
- Small leaf (optional)
- Lightweight cardboard
- Acrylic paint
- Foam paintbrush

### START TO FINISH

STEP 1. Draw or trace a leaf onto the cardboard, then cut it out. Trace the shape several times onto the nonsticky side of wide painter's tape; cut out. Stick the tape leaves to the shade and seal the edges with a rigid plastic card. (To help with the placement of the leaves, set the shade on a lighted lamp while you work. The light will help you determine whether the leaves are evenly spaced.)

STEP 2. Using long, even strokes, paint the shade with two coats of acrylic paint. After the paint dries, place the shade on a lighted lamp and check for streaks or thin spots. Touch up the paint as needed.

STEP 3. After the paint dries, carefully peel away the tape as *below*. When the light is turned on, the white leaves will glow against the opaque background.

## 38 Candle Makers

### MATERIALS
- Plain candle shade with follower hardware (available at crafts and decorating stores)
- Decorative paper napkin
- Spray adhesive
- Pencil
- Scissors

### START TO FINISH

STEP 1. Drape the napkin over the shade, making the most of border patterns. Mark the points where the napkin overlaps to create straight seams. (The napkin pattern may not align at the seam.) Mark the top edge of the shade. Cut the napkin on the marked lines, adding a ½-inch overlap at the seam line.

STEP 2. Spray the shade with adhesive, following the manufacturer's directions. Smooth the napkin in place over the shade.

NOTE: For safety, remove a paper shade when burning a candle.

## lamp&lighting tips

Don't underestimate the proper placement of lighting, which can prevent eyestrain and headaches. Follow this general rule: The diameter of the beam spread out of the bottom of the shade for reading and writing should be about 16 inches. At a desk, work lamps should be 15 inches above the desk's surface, whether mounted on the wall or sitting on the desk.

### TOO BIG?

Table lamps should not tower above the furniture. Choose a lamp that will provide optimal reading light when seated, which means you shouldn't see the bulb and its annoying casting glare.

### TOO SMALL?

Be careful not to let a petite lamp be overwhelmed by a high-back sofa or stocky chair. A small lamp may also function less than adequately, since optimum reading light comes from slightly above eye level.

### BULB BASICS

INCANDESCENT. These bulbs cast a warm, pleasant light and show fabrics and paints in their true colors, but can make the room uncomfortably warm if too many are used in several lamps.

FLUORESCENT. Compact versions that fit standard fixtures cost more than incandescents but use only one-third the electricity. For kitchens, choose warm white (not cool white) tubes for the best color.

TUNGSTEN-HALOGEN. This low-voltage incandescent bulb provides an intense beam that's ideal for spotlighting objects. The bulbs last longer and use less electricity than standard incandescents, but cost more upfront and produce lots of heat.

# window wizardry

## 43 Side Treatment

**MATERIALS**

- Plain pique or linenlike drapery panels
- 1½-inch-wide sheer ribbon cut into 27-inch strips
- Purchased ribbon daisies
- Fabric glue, or hot-glue gun and glue sticks

**START TO FINISH**

STEP 1. Press the rod pocket smooth. Fold the ribbon strips in half crosswise and machine-sew the fold to the wrong side of the upper edge of the panel. Start 1 inch from each side edge and evenly space the ribbons about 8 inches apart.

STEP 2. Glue on ribbon daisies.

NOTE: Adding ribbon ties will lengthen the curtain. Hanging the rod higher so the curtain does not pool on the floor makes the window appear larger and more open.

## 44 Sheer Magic

**MATERIALS**

- Purchased drapery panels and sheer fabric
- Wide upholstery cord with a flange for sewing
- Narrow upholstery cord for ties

**START TO FINISH**

STEP 1. Cut two sheer panels 30 inches wide and as long as the width of the drapery panels plus hem allowances. (If necessary, shorten the drapery panels to allow for the sheers.)

STEP 2. Hem the narrow ends of the sheer panels. Press under ½ inch, then 3 inches on the top edge of each sheer panel. Topstitch along the lower folded edge to form the top hem.

STEP 3. Baste wide cord along the top edge of each drapery panel. Using a zipper foot and a ½-inch seam allowance, sew each sheer panel to a drapery panel close to the cording. Press the seam allowances toward the drapery panels.

STEP 4. To form hanging loops, make a pair of 1-inch-long vertical buttonholes side by side, spacing them 1 inch apart. Evenly space pairs of buttonholes across top of sheer panels, approximately every 12 inches.

STEP 5. Cut the narrow cord into 18-inch lengths. Knot one end of a cord. Thread the other end from front to back through the left buttonhole of a pair, over the rod, and from back to front through the right buttonhole. Knot that end. Tie the ends of the cord together. Repeat for each pair of buttonholes.

## 45 Casual or Formal

**MATERIALS**

- Plain cotton or muslin panels with tab tops
- ⅝- and ⅜-inch-wide matching ribbons
- Fade-out fabric marker and ruler
- Fusing tape, fusing liquid, fabric glue, or sewing thread to match the ribbon
- Fray-check liquid
- Buttons to match the ribbon

**START TO FINISH**

STEP 1. Cut the ribbons to fit the side and bottom edges of the panels. Mark the placement line for the wider ribbon ¾ inch from each edge. Fuse or sew the ribbon along the marked lines, butting the joints at the corners. (The ribbon will stand up to washing better if sewn.) Treat each cut edge with fray-check liquid and turn the upper ends to the back side of panel.

STEP 2. Mark the line for the narrower ribbon ¼ inch from the first ribbon band. Sew or fuse the ribbon in place in the same manner.

STEP 3. Sew a button at the base of each tab.

## 46 Dyed Design

**MATERIALS**

- Plain drapery panels
- Mustard
- Red paste food coloring (optional)
- White vinegar
- Microwave-safe bag

**START TO FINISH**

STEP 1. Silk and wool fabrics work best for this project. Wash and dry the panels. Iron the fabric and tape it tautly to a paper-covered work surface.

STEP 2. Shake the mustard and apply it in spirals directly to the fabric (*photo 1, page 236*). (For better contrast, darken the mustard by adding a smidgen of red paste food coloring to the container.) Let the mustard set for about 30 minutes until it's nearly dry. Rinse the fabric with a high-powered spray of warm water until the mustard is dislodged and the water runs clear.

# window wizardry

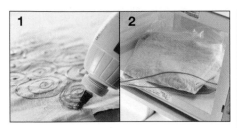

STEP 3. To set the color, immerse the fabric in 10 quarts of warm water and 1 cup of vinegar, agitating it to remove the excess mustard. Seal the wet fabric inside a microwave-safe plastic bag and turn on at 50 percent power for five minutes (*photo 2*.) Watch the fabric carefully so it doesn't scorch.

STEP 4. Line-dry the fabric; press with an iron to further set the design. (Clothes dryers do not get hot enough to set a dye.)

## 48 Bygone Times
MATERIALS
- Purchased sheer panel
- Ball fringe
- Grommets and grommet tool (either plier-type or hammer-type)
- Fray-check liquid (optional)

### START TO FINISH
STEP 1. Cut the panel in half to form two panels. Hem the raw edges, turning under ½ inch, then ½ inch again. Topstitch the ball fringe over the hems, turning under the raw edge of the flange. You may want to treat this edge with fray-check liquid.

STEP 2. Mark the points for the grommets along the curtain top, starting about 1 inch from each edge and evenly spacing the grommets about 8 inches apart. Following the package

directions, use a grommet tool to place a grommet at each mark, going through all the fabric layers.

NOTES: Make sure the grommets are large enough and the rod is small enough that the curtain panels slide easily. Look for rods and tiebacks that repeat the ball design for a unified look.

## 50 Stamp of Approval
MATERIALS
- Lightly tinted sheer swag and side panels
- Stamp and ink pad designed for use on fabric
- Kraft paper
- Low-tack painter's tape
- Press cloth

### START TO FINISH
STEP 1. Prewash and dry the swag and panels to remove any sizing or finishes. Do not use any laundry products that contain fabric softener or stain repellent. Lightly press the fabric if needed.

STEP 2. Smoothly tape one section of a side panel to a paper-covered work surface, taking care not to distort the fabric. Using even pressure, randomly stamp the fabric without rocking the stamp. As each section is stamped, change paper and move to another section. Repeat for the other panel.

STEP 3. To create the border on the swag, mask off 1 inch at the lower edge. Place the swag over kraft paper and press the stamp directly onto the fabric. Move along the edge, letting the color look mottled and uneven.

STEP 4. When the ink dries, cover the fabric with a press cloth and heat-set the designs according to the stamp-pad manufacturer's directions.

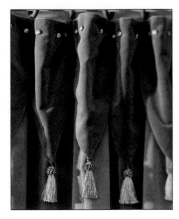

## 53 Tassel Toppers
MATERIALS
- Velvet drapery fabric
- Lining to match the velvet
- Small upholstery tassels
- Satin-covered buttons
- Paper for pattern

### START TO FINISH
STEP 1. Measure the width and length of the existing drapery. To determine the width of each point, choose a measurement that divides evenly into the drapery width. The length of the points should be approximately one-sixth the length of the drapery panel. To make the pattern for the points, draw a line as long as the width measurement (for example, 6 inches for a 48-inch panel divided into eight points). Intersect this line with a line as long as the length measurement (for example, 12 inches for a 72-inch-long drapery panel) to form a T. Join the ends of the lines to form a triangle. Add ½ inch seam allowances. Cut out pattern.

STEP 2. Cut the points from the velvet and lining fabrics. With right sides facing, sew around the triangles, leaving a small opening at the top for turning. Clip the corners and turn the triangle right side out. Slip-stitch the opening closed.

STEP 3. Evenly space and tack the triangles over the drapery panel. Sew a satin-covered button over each tacked spot. Sew a small tassel to the end of each point.

# window wizardry

## 54 Coordination Counts

**MATERIALS**

- Two pairs of unlined drapery panels in coordinating patterns
- Contrasting fabric for the band
- Two buttons

**START TO FINISH**

STEP 1. If the panels are not the same size, trim them to match. With wrong sides facing, baste the panels together in pairs along the outer edges.

STEP 2. Cut 5-inch-wide binding strips for the sides and bottom of each panel, piecing as necessary. Cut 5-inch-wide strips to form the panel casings. Add 1-inch hem allowance to the side of each casing.

STEP 3. Fold the binding strips in half, right sides out; press. Open, and press under ½ inch on long edges. Sew a raw long edge of each binding strip to the front of a panel, right sides facing. Miter the corners. Turn the binding to the back, encasing the raw edges. Topstitch close to the fold. Turn under the raw edges at the top corners of the panel. Slip-stitch the mitered corners closed.

STEP 4. Hem the short ends of each top casing. Sew a casing strip to the top of each panel in the same manner as the binding strips, leaving the ends open to insert the curtain rod.

STEP 5. Hang the curtains. Sew a button to the outside edge of each panel at the same height as the windowsill. Take down the curtain and make a buttonhole directly opposite the button on the inner edge. Rehang the curtain. To open the curtain, button the inner edge to the outer edge.

## 55 Paper Pockets

**MATERIALS**

- Roughly textured paper
- Wood dowels
- Dried flowers
- Hooks
- Needle

**START TO FINISH**

STEP 1. Choose a paper that has a rough texture, similar to lightweight nonwoven interfacing. Most art papers are sold in sheets with narrow widths, so save this project for a small window.

STEP 2. Cut the paper so it covers the glass and the window's sash, adding 4 inches to the length for the rod pockets. Fold over and stitch or glue 2-inch rod pockets at the top and bottom. Cut two ½-inch-wide wood dowels as long as the window sash and insert them into the rod pockets. Cut paper rectangles for flower pockets. Center pockets over individual windowpanes, and glue or stitch in place with long running stitches. Tuck dried flowers inside each pocket. Avoid overhandling the fragile paper.

STEP 3. Screw hooks into the upper corners of the window. With a large needle, poke a hole aligned with the hooks in each upper corner of the curtain so the hook can cradle the dowel. Hang the curtain on the hooks.

## 56 Same but Different

**MATERIALS**

- Valance fabric deep enough to cover one-third to one-half of the window and wide enough to swag gently and drape at the ends (include hem allowances; fabric amount will vary according to fabric weight and window size)
- Coordinating fabric for the ruffled trim
- Ring tape and cord for Roman shades

**START TO FINISH**

STEP 1. Narrowly hem the bottom and both side edges of valance fabric. Make a rod pocket in the top edge. Hang the valance and mark the inside edge of the window frame. Sew the ring tape to the back of the valance along the marked lines. Tie the center of a cord to each bottom ring. Run one end of cord through the rings and leave the other free.

STEP 2. Cut a ruffle strip three times the measurement of the lower edge of the valance and double the depth of the finished ruffle, adding seam allowances, and piecing as necessary. Fold the ruffle strip in half lengthwise, right sides facing. Sew across the short ends. Turn to the right side and press. Baste the raw edges together. Gather the raw edges tightly and sew to the bottom of the valance. Clean-finish the seam at the bottom edge with zigzag stitches, or serge and press the seam allowance toward the window valance.

STEP 3. Rehang the valance. Draw up the cords to create the swag and tie the ends to the top ring.

# window wizardry

## 57 Paper Penny-Pinchers

### MATERIALS

- Towel bar holders
- Towel bar long enough to span the window, or painted wooden dowel cut to size
- Lacy art paper
- Hole punch
- Narrow satin ribbon

### START TO FINISH

STEP 1. Mount a towel bar holder on each side of the window about halfway down the window. Insert the towel bar or dowel into the holders.

STEP 2. Measure the length of the bar. Cut two pieces of lacy art paper each a few inches wider than half the bar length and long enough to drape over the bar to the sill in back and two-thirds of the way to the sill in front.

STEP 3. Drape the paper over the bar to make café curtains. Make sure bottom edges are level. Pinch about an inch of curtain a few inches below the bar, catching both the front and back layers. Punch a hole through all the pinched layers. Tie a length of narrow satin ribbon through the holes, forming a pleat, *below.* Repeat the pleats every 4–5 inches.

## 58 In the Swing

### MATERIALS

- Four swing-arm rods
- Decorative art paper
- Straightedge
- Hole punch
- Raffia ribbon

### START TO FINISH

STEP 1. Mount a pair of swing-arm rods right side up about halfway down the window frame, following the manufacturer's instructions. Mount the second pair upside down at the bottom of the window.

STEP 2. To create the paper panels, measure the area between the rods. Subtract ½–1 inch from the length so a small space will remain between the panels and rods. Use a pencil to transfer the measurements to the art paper. Lay the straightedge on each drawn line. Holding the straightedge firmly in place, carefully pull up the paper along the straightedge to tear the excess paper away.

STEP 3. Punch holes about ½ inch from the edge and about 1 inch apart along the top and bottom edges of the paper panels. Thread raffia ribbon through the holes and around the top rods, leaving a small space between the paper panels and rods, as *above.* Tie off. Repeat with bottom rods, pulling the paper panels taut.

## 60 Bead Works

### MATERIALS

- Fabric deep enough to cover one-third to one-half of the window and wide enough to swag gently and drape at the ends (also allow for hems; fabric amount will vary according to fabric weight and window size)
- Ring tape and cord for Roman shades
- Acrylic beaded trim for bottom edge

### START TO FINISH

STEP 1. Narrowly hem the bottom and both side edges. Make a rod pocket in the top edge. Hang the valance in the window and mark the inside edge of the window frame. Sew the ring tape to the back of the valance along the marked lines. Tie the center of a cord to each bottom ring. Run one end of cord through the rings and leave the other free.

STEP 2. Sew the beaded trim to the bottom edge of the valance, turning under the raw edges at each end. Rehang the valance. Draw up the cords to create the swag and tie the ends to the top ring.

# window wizardry

## 61 Case Study

**MATERIALS**
- Set of floral ruffle-hem pillowcases
- Set of white cutwork-edge pillowcases
- 6⅔ total yards of 1-inch-wide grosgrain ribbon in two coordinating colors
- 1¼ yards of 1-inch-wide white grosgrain ribbon

**START TO FINISH**
STEP 1. Lay a floral ruffle-hem pillowcase on a flat work surface. Position a white cutwork-edge pillowcase over the floral pillowcase so the ruffle extends below the open end of the white pillowcase. If necessary, trim the pillowcases even at the closed end. Slip the floral pillowcase inside the white pillowcase. Repeat with the remaining pillowcases.
STEP 2. To make ties to hang the curtain, cut a 2-foot length from each of the two coordinating-color ribbons. Layer the two ribbons, and sew along the long edges. Cut a V in each end. Repeat to make a total of 10 ties.
STEP 3. Fold each tie in half crosswise. In each top corner of the paired pillowcases, position a folded tie, slightly overlapping the tie in front of the pillowcases. Equally space other ties in between; baste.
STEP 4. Cut the white ribbon in half. Position a white ribbon length along the top edge of each set of paired pillowcases to finish the edge and cover folded tie ends. Turn under short ends of the white ribbon. Sew along the long edges of the white ribbon through all layers, catching the ties in the stitching.
STEP 5. To hang, tie the ribbons to a curtain rod, allowing excess ribbon to drape over the curtain rod.

## 62 No Peeking

**MATERIALS**
- Window film, such as Wallpaper for Windows
- Spray water bottle and liquid soap
- Towel
- Squeegee

**START TO FINISH**
STEP 1. Measure the width and height of the glass surface you want to cover. Subtract ¼ inch from these measurements. Use scissors or a crafts knife to cut a piece of window film to these measurements.
STEP 2. Make sure the glass is clean and free of film or grease. Mix a few drops of soap with water in a spray bottle. Place a towel at the base of the window to catch drips. Wet the glass surface.
STEP 2. Peel the film from its backing paper; position it on the wet glass. Spray the film-covered glass with the diluted soap, and beginning at the top, use a squeegee to smooth out air bubbles, as *below*. Reposition the window film if necessary.

## 63 Mirror, Mirror

**MATERIALS**
- Plain mirror without bevels
- Paper for pattern (optional)
- Black transfer paper
- Flexible adhesive-backed leading strips (available at crafts stores)
- Crafts knife
- Simulated liquid leading (available at crafts stores)
- Transparent glass paint
- Small artist's brush
- Foam-core board
- Wire gallery clips

**START TO FINISH**
STEP 1. Plan a design to fit your mirror (our mirror is 18x24 inches). Use the pencil to draw the design on paper to make a pattern, if desired.
STEP 2. Place the mirror on a level work surface. Make sure the mirror is clean and free of film or grease. Transfer the design from the paper to the mirror using a pencil and black transfer paper.
STEP 3. Press the leading strips onto the design lines on the mirror. Use the crafts knife to cut the leading strips to the lengths needed; do not overlap them. When all the leading strips are positioned, fill any gaps with the simulated liquid leading; let dry.

# window wizardry

STEP 4. Paint the mirror between the leading lines using transparent glass paint in colors of your choice and a small artist's brush. Use the bottle tip to add texture to the paint as shown *above left*. Apply additional coats of transparent glass paint to intensify the color. Let the paint dry for a minimum of 24 hours.

STEP 5. Cut a piece of foam-core board to the size of the mirror. Mount the mirror on foam-core board with wire gallery clips, *above right*.

## 64 Can-Do Curtain
MATERIALS
- Lace, such as an old tablecloth or inexpensive lace fabric
- Stencil adhesive
- Kraft paper
- Low-tack painter's tape
- White enamel spray paint

### START TO FINISH

STEP 1. Measure the width and height of the glass surface you want to cover. Use these measurements to cut a piece of lace. Make sure the glass is clean and free of film or grease.

STEP 2. Spray one side of the lace with stencil adhesive. Center the lace on the glass with the adhesive side down. Press the lace onto the glass, smoothing out wrinkles.

STEP 3. Mask off the window edges with kraft paper and painter's tape. Holding the spray-paint can upright several inches from the glass, spray a light coat of white paint over the lace with slow, steady strokes. When dry, apply a second light coat. Remove the lace, kraft paper, and tape. NOTE: Avoid doing this project on cold or humid days because icy or sweating glass resists paint.

## 70 Towel Time
MATERIALS
- Tea towels
- 1x2 wooden board
- ½-inch plastic curtain rings
- ¼-inch dowel
- Shade-and-blind cord
- Screw eyes
- Fabric glue
- Cleat

### START TO FINISH

STEP 1. To make shades long enough for your windows, overlap narrow hems on short sides of towels and sew together.

STEP 2. Stitch plastic curtain rings to the long, hemmed edges on the wrong side of the towels. Sew the first ring 7 inches from the top of the towel, and the last ring 2 to 5 inches from the bottom hem. Space rings in between about every 5 inches, making sure they're even side to side. See illustration, *right*.

STEP 3. For mounting and stability, cut the wood board and dowel to width of shade. Slide dowel through bottom rings and glue ends to towel. Staple top of the shade to a 2-inch side of the board. On the other 2-inch side, twist small screw eyes in line with each row of rings.

STEP 4. Cut a piece of shade-and-blind cord for each row of rings. Cut one cord to double the length of the shade; the other cord should be that length plus the width. Determine what side you want the string control on, and tie the short cord to the bottom ring on this side. Tie the longer cord to the other bottom ring. Secure with fabric glue. Run each cord through the rings directly above it and through all the screw eyes across the board, as *below*. Both strings come out the same eye. Trim the cord ends to be even and tie them together.

STEP 5. For inside mounting, staple the fabric-stapled side of board against the upper window frame; screw in place.

STEP 6. Screw a small cleat to the side of the window. To raise the shade, pull cords evenly and loop around cleat.

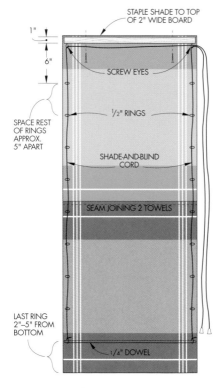

STAPLE SHADE TO TOP OF 2" WIDE BOARD

1"

6"

SCREW EYES

½" RINGS

SPACE REST OF RINGS APPROX. 5" APART

SHADE-AND-BLIND CORD

SEAM JOINING 2 TOWELS

LAST RING 2"–5" FROM BOTTOM

¼" DOWEL

# window wizardry

## 71 International View

### MATERIALS

- Fusible shade kit
- Paper map large enough to cover your window or windows
- Pressing cloth

### START TO FINISH

STEP 1. Trim roller tube and fusible backing from shade kit to fit your window, following the manufacturer's instructions. Lay the map right side down on a large work surface. Position fusible backing on the map, centering as desired. (If you are making two shades from one map, place the two fusible backings side by side to be sure the maps will line up when shades are hung.) Trace around the backing on the map. Cut map to size.

STEP 2. Using a pressing cloth to protect the paper, fuse the map to the fusible backing, following the manufacturer's instructions. Fold up 2 inches at the bottom of the shade for the hem, *below*. Use the shade kit's fusible tape to fuse the hem in place. Insert the kit's slat in the hem. Attach shade to roller tube. Install shade hardware; hang shade.

## 73 New Country

### MATERIALS

- 1x4-inch pine board slightly wider than the window for the mounting board
- Doorknobs (enough to be spaced every 12 inches plus two for tiebacks)
- Dowels to fit the shank of the doorknobs
- Drill with countersink bit
- Bolts
- Wooden plugs
- Paint
- Drapery panels totaling 1½ times the width of the mounting board

### START TO FINISH

STEP 1. Paint the mounting board. Cut a dowel to fit the shank of each doorknob and to extend ½ inch beyond the shank. Countersink the knob onto the board and secure it with a countersunk screw from the back. Bolt the board to the wall, centering it over the window. Countersink the bolts and fill the holes with wooden plugs. Touch up paint.

STEP 2. In the panels, make buttonholes large enough to insert the doorknobs, spacing them 18 inches apart. (The buttonholes shown are approximately 3 inches long.) Loop the buttonholes over the doorknobs, as *below*.

STEP 3. Mount a doorknob on each side of the window for tiebacks, placing about three-quarters of the way down the window frame.

## 75 Piping Hot

### MATERIALS

- Sheer polyester or polyester-blend fabric, enough to measure 1½ times the width of the window and at least two-thirds the depth of the window (fabric amount will vary according to window size)
- Dark-color piping
- Tassels to match piping
- Paper for patterns
- Water-erasable fabric marker
- Three tieback brackets

### START TO FINISH

NOTE: This valance is made from a double layer of the same fabric. Piping is sandwiched between two layers, and the fold of the fabric forms the upper edge.

STEP 1. Fold the fabric in half, right sides facing. Set it aside while making the pattern.

STEP 2. To make the pattern, mark the width of the valance (1½ times the width of the window). Mark points at the desired depth. Leave the top and side edges straight, and draw a gently swooping line through the points on the lower edge (see *above*). When you are satisfied with the pattern, transfer it to the fabric. Place the top edge of the pattern along the fold, and mark the remaining edges. Baste the piping along the marked lines of one layer of the valance fabric, turning under raw edges. Using a zipper foot, sew through all layers along the marked lines and against the piping, leaving an opening for turning. Trim away the excess fabric and turn the valance to the right side. Slip-stitch the opening closed. Tack a tassel to each fabric point.

## window wizardry

STEP 3. Cut three 1x12-inch ties from the fabric scraps. Fold the ties in half lengthwise and sew along all the raw edges, leaving an opening for turning. Turn the ties to the right side and slip-stitch the opening closed. Fold the ties in half crosswise and tack at the outer edges and center of the valance top.

STEP 4. Attach the tiebacks to the wall directly over the window trim at the outer edges and center of the window. Tie the valance to the tiebacks.

### 80 Sign of the Times
MATERIALS
- An odd number of napkins in two coordinating patterns, one light and one dark
- Two more napkin rings than napkins
- Narrow curtain rod and mounting brackets

START TO FINISH
STEP 1. Mount the brackets at the top of the window. Slide the rings onto the rod and put the rod in place.
STEP 2. Fold the napkins in half diagonally. Starting with the darker napkins for the background, slip the napkin ends through the even-numbered napkin rings. Tuck the ends of the remaining napkins through the odd-numbered rings. Adjust the cloth so that some of the tails extend beyond the rings and swag slightly. If necessary, tack the napkins to the rings on the back side.

### 85 Campfire Retreat
MATERIALS
- Old metal coffeepot
- Metal primer (optional)
- Sandpaper (optional)
- Acrylic paints in yellow, blue, and white
- Paintbrushes: 1-inch foam, flat, and liner
- Water-base spray sealer

START TO FINISH
STEP 1. The coffeepot above was white with rust showing through before the plaid design was added. If your coffeepot is not white, apply metal primer. After it dries, paint the piece white. If you want some rust to show through, lightly sand the paint in random areas. If your coffeepot is rusty and you do not want rust to show through, prime the metal and paint it white as described above. Do not sand the finish.
STEP 2. Mix blue and white 2:1. Thin the paint with water until it is the consistency of ink. Paint wide vertical stripes around the pot using a foam brush and spacing the stripes fairly evenly.
STEP 3. Using undiluted blue and a liner brush, paint a thin stripe to the left of each wide stripe. Let the paint dry.
STEP 4. Mix yellow and white 1:1. Thin the paint with water until it is the consistency of ink. Using the flat brush, paint horizontal stripes around the coffeepot, spacing the lines fairly evenly.
STEP 5. After the paint is dry, seal it with spray sealer.

### 86 Yipes, Stripes!
MATERIALS
- Large galvanized tub
- Low-tack painter's tape
- Sandpaper and tack cloth
- Metal primer
- Blue and white enamel paints

START TO FINISH
STEP 1. Clean the tub thoroughly. Mask off the upper portion of the tub. Lightly sand below the tape and wipe the bucket clean. Paint the sanded area with metal primer, then two or more coats of white enamel paint, letting dry after each coat.
STEP 2. Divide the circumference of the tub into an even number of stripes. Tape off the stripes and paint the masked sections blue. Remove the tape.

# containers for all

## 88 Weaved Wire

**MATERIALS**

- 16-gauge black wire
- 24-gauge black wire
- Glass vase

**START TO FINISH**

STEP 1. Fold thirty 12-inch strips of 16-gauge black wire in half.

STEP 2. Line up wire strips on a table with the folded ends extending 1½ inches past the edge. Lay a piece of scrap wood on top and clamp to secure.

STEP 3. Wrap one end of a 2-foot-long 24-gauge black wire around the looped end of the last folded wire, then weave the wire over and under the remaining wires. Weave two more fine wires in the same way (see *below*).

STEP 4. Loosen the clamps and move wires to extend 4 inches off the table. Reclamp.

STEP 5. Weave three more wires.

STEP 6. Wrap woven wires around a 4-inch-tall glass cylinder vase; secure by twisting pairs of fine wires together.

STEP 7. Trim and bend tops of heavier wire at random.

## 92 Up Against the Fence

**MATERIALS**

- Galvanized buckets
- Low-tack painter's tape
- Sandpaper and tack cloth
- Metal primer
- Enamel paint
- Drill with ⅜-inch bit (optional)
- Cup hooks (optional)

**START TO FINISH**

STEP 1. Clean the buckets thoroughly. Mask off the upper one-third of each bucket. Lightly sand below the tape and wipe the bucket clean. Paint the sanded area with metal primer, then two or more coats of enamel paint, letting each coat dry before applying the next coat.

STEP 2. To hang buckets that do not have hanging holes or handles, drill a ⅜-inch hole 1 inch from the top edge. Hang the buckets from small cup hooks.

## 93 Pull Up a Seat

**MATERIALS**

- Old chair with small rim for supporting the box or strapping bands across the seat
- 1x4-inch pine board
- Exterior-grade plywood scrap
- Wood glue
- Nails
- Clamps
- Drill
- Exterior-grade wood sealer
- Window screen scrap

**START TO FINISH**

STEP 1. Cut the 1x4-inch pine to make a box that fits inside the chair seat. Glue and nail the corners using butt joints, and clamp the joints until the glue dries. Cut a base from exterior-grade plywood. Glue and nail it to the frame. Drill drainage holes through the bottom.

STEP 2. Seal the box with exterior-grade sealer. Line the bottom with window screen before adding soil.

# marvelous moldings

## 94 Out on a Ledge

MATERIALS

- Wide crown molding
- 1x2-inch pine board
- L-shape brackets
- Small wood screws
- Toggle bolts or similar fasteners
- Finishing nails
- Wood glue
- Paint
- Level
- Wood filler

START TO FINISH

STEP 1. For frame front, cut molding to the desired length, mitering the ends at a 45-degree angle. (The shelves shown are 4 feet long.) For frame sides, cut two small molding pieces, mitering one end of each. Glue and nail molding pieces together.

STEP 2. Cut the 1x2 to form a shelf that fits in the molding frame with its top edge slightly below the frame's top edge, creating a lip to keep display items in place. Paint the molding frame and the shelf. (The color shown was created by brushing diluted white paint over the wood and wiping away the excess paint.)

STEP 3. Using a level, mark a straight line on the wall for the placement of the shelf piece. Attach the shelf to the wall using L-brackets, wood screws, and toggle bolts. Position the molding frame on the shelf and nail it in place. Countersink the nails and fill holes, then touch up the paint.

## 96 Console Yourself

MATERIALS

- Vintage or reproduction corbels
- Pine board for the shelf
- Latex paints in rust, white, gold, and black; or in colors to match your vintage corbel
- Paintbrushes and rags
- Old toothbrush or flecking tool
- Finishing nails
- Screws
- Polyurethane
- Wood filler

START TO FINISH

STEP 1. Cut the board to the proper size for the shelf. (This will depend on the corbel and room size.) Paint the shelf. To match a vintage corbel, carefully study the colors and layers of paint on the corbel. Apply similarly colored paint to the board, working to replicate the layers and textures of the paint. The match will not be exact, just blended. To age new corbels and boards, brush each piece with a layer of rust-color paint. Dilute the white paint with an equal amount of water. Paint the pieces white, then lightly wipe away the excess paint with a rag. Randomly brush on stripes of white paint and gold paint. Blend the paint with a rag to eliminate harsh edges. Dip a toothbrush or flecking tool into the black paint. Pull back the bristles to fleck black paint onto the surface. Let the paint dry.

STEP 2. Position the corbels on the wall ¾ inch lower than the finished shelf will be. If possible, place the corbels against wall studs. Holding your drill at an angle, screw through the top of the corbel and into the wall in two or more places. To hold the lower end of the corbel in place, nail throughout the corbel and into the wall. If possible, pick an inconspicuous spot for the nails. Drilling pilot holes for the nails will help prevent the wood from splitting.

STEP 3. Center the shelf over the corbels. Screw the shelf to the corbels through the top, countersinking the screws or nails. Fill all nail and screw holes and retouch the paint. Seal with polyurethane.

## 97 High and Dry

MATERIALS

- 1x8 pine board
- Stemware molding (available ready-made at lumber stores)
- Paint
- Wood glue
- Finishing nails
- Clamps
- Screws
- Wood filler

START TO FINISH

STEP 1. Enlarge the pattern *opposite* to scale. Cut two brackets for each rack from the 1x8 pine. Also cut a 6x32-inch shelf for the small rack and a 7¼x48-inch shelf for the large rack. Position the brackets on the underside of the shelves, placing them 3 inches from each end and flush with the back. Glue, clamp, and nail them in place.

# marvelous moldings

STEP 2. Cut the stemware molding into seven 5-inch pieces for the small rack and eleven 6-inch pieces for the large rack. For each rack, cut a left edge from one molding piece and a right edge from another so these pieces will fit flush against the brackets. Paint the shelves, brackets, and all molding strips. Place the cut edges of the end strips at the ends of each shelf, facing the brackets. Glue and nail them in place.

STEP 3. Evenly space the full molding pieces flush with the back edge of the shelf, center-spaced 3¾ inches apart. Glue and nail the pieces in place.

STEP 4. Mark a level line on the wall where the top of the shelf will be placed. Drill screws at an angle through the top of the shelf and into the wall studs. Fill all holes and retouch the paint.

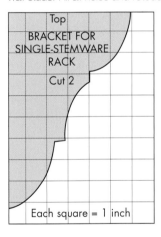

Top
BRACKET FOR SINGLE-STEMWARE RACK
Cut 2

Each square = 1 inch

## 98 Faux Facade

### MATERIALS

- 1x6 poplar ripped to 4 inches wide
- Standard windowsill
- Colonial casing
- Quarter-round molding
- Screen molding
- Chair rail
- Wood glue
- Screws
- Finishing nails
- Wood filler
- Wallpaper and wallpaper hanging supplies
- Paint

### START TO FINISH

STEP 1. Draw the outside dimensions of the plate rack onto the wall, then wallpaper inside these lines. The bottom of the rack should be about 32 inches from the floor.

STEP 2. Build the outer frame from the poplar strips. Cut windowsill stock for the shelves and nail them to the frame, allowing enough space between each piece for the plates you plan to display. Tack a strip of screen molding onto the top of each windowsill piece 2½ inches from the back to make a lip to hold the plates in place. Paint the rack; let dry. Mount rack to the wall by angling screws through the sills and into wall studs.

STEP 3. Cut quarter-round molding and colonial casing to fit the shelves; paint each piece and let dry. Nail colonial casing to underside of each shelf, aligning the back edges. Nail quarter-round molding to front edge of shelves.

STEP 4. Paint the chair-rail pieces; let dry. Mark

a horizontal line even with the bottom of the plate rack. Wallpaper to this line. Attach the chair rail at the rack base, covering the wallpaper edge.

STEP 5. Fill all nail and screw holes and retouch paint.

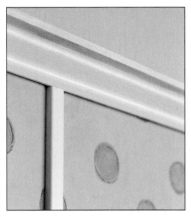

## 99 Divide and Conquer

### MATERIALS

- ⁷⁄₁₆x⅜-inch door stop
- ⁷⁄₁₆x1¼-inch custom molding (undercap)
- ¼x¾-inch screen molding
- Nails: No. 6 finishing and nail brads
- All-purpose glue
- Wood filler
- Paints
- Wallpaper and hanging supplies (optional)

### START TO FINISH

STEP 1. The height of the horizontal molding will vary according to ceiling height. At desired height, draw a line along the wall using a level. Apply wallpaper or a painted finish below the line.

STEP 2. Cut screen molding to fit vertically from marked line to baseboard. Drill pilot holes to prevent the wood from splitting. Paint all molding pieces; let dry.

STEP 3. Space the screen-molding strips about 24 inches apart, and glue to the wall. Secure with brads while the glue dries. Nail the custom molding over the vertical strips. Drill pilot holes, and nail No. 6 finishing nails into wall studs.

STEP 4. Glue the door stop to the top of the custom molding. Hold it in place with small nails until the glue dries. Fill all nail holes and retouch the paint.

# marvelous moldings

### 100 Top It Off

MATERIALS

- Purchased or handmade brackets
- 1x4 pine board
- Narrow decorative molding for shelf trim
- Tension rods
- Screws
- Finishing nails
- Wood glue
- Wood filler
- Paint

START TO FINISH

STEP 1. Cut the 1x4 and molding pieces to the proper size. The shelf should extend beyond the window frame 1 to 2 inches on each side. Attach decorative molding to shelf edges. Paint all pieces, including the brackets; let dry.

STEP 2. Hold the shelf in place against the wall with the underside against the top of the window frame. Mark a line on the underside of the shelf where the front edge of the window frame meets the shelf. Place back edge of the brackets even with this line 1 inch in from each end. This should leave a notch that will fit over the window frame, and the shelf should extend just past the front of the brackets. Glue and screw the brackets to the shelf. Large windows need a third bracket in the center to prevent the shelf from sagging.

STEP 3. Holding the shelf in place, drive screws from the top directly into the window frame. If more support is needed, insert screws at an angle through the brackets and into the window frame. Fill all the nail and screw holes and retouch the paint. Place tension rods between the brackets to hold the valance or the curtain.

### 101 Framed!

MATERIALS

- ½-inch-thick cork panels
- 1-inch-wide cherry trim (other wood may be substituted)
- Pictures
- All-purpose glue
- Finishing nails
- Wood filler to match wood trim

START TO FINISH

STEP 1. Cut the cork into 12-inch-wide strips. Glue cork to the wall directly above the cabinets. Cut top and bottom trim pieces to match the width of the cabinets. Glue and nail the trim pieces over the cork, leaving 10 inches of exposed cork between the strips. Cut side pieces to fit between top and bottom strips. Glue and nail the side strips in place. Fill nail holes.

STEP 2. Pin pictures to the cork, trimming slightly if needed.

## unusual tables

### 103 Form and Function

MATERIALS

- Four large finials with square bases (available at home improvement stores as tops for fence posts or newels)
- Landscape timber or other lumber to fit the finial base
- Glass for tabletop
- Wood glue
- Black spray paint
- Clear silicone adhesive

START TO FINISH

STEP 1. Measure the finial. Cut four timber bases so that the final height of the bases plus the finials equals 18 to 20 inches. Most lumberyards will cut the lumber for a nominal charge. Glue each finial to a base. Paint the bases black; let dry.

STEP 2. Set the bases in place, and measure the size of the glass you will need. Have a glass supply store cut your tabletop to size. For safety, have the top cut with "dime cut" (slightly rounded) edges and use glass that is at least ⅜ inch thick.

STEP 3. Place a dab of clear silicone on the very top of each finial, and set the glass in place.

# unusual tables

## 104 Excess Baggage

**MATERIALS**

- Graduated vintage or reproduction suitcases (they do not have to match but should be made of the same material)
- Good-quality leather cleaner (optional)
- Baking soda or charcoal briquettes (optional)

**START TO FINISH**

STEP 1. Carefully clean the suitcases. For leather suitcases, polish the leather to prevent it from drying out. If the suitcases smell musty, sprinkle them with baking soda and set them outside in the sun for several hours. If they still have a slight odor, place a few charcoal briquettes in each suitcase. They eventually absorb most odors.

STEP 2. Stack the suitcases from large to small.

## 105 Gingerbread Cutout

**MATERIALS**

- Circular table and glass tabletop
- Wood
- Paper for pattern
- Quick-release spray adhesive
- Drill with small bit
- Scroll saw
- Sandpaper and tack cloth
- Paint

**START TO FINISH**

NOTE: If you've never operated a scroll saw, practice cutting scrap material before you begin a fretwork project like this. You need to saw straight lines, curves, corners, and acute angles.

STEP 1. Enlarge the pattern *right* to fit your table; cut it out. Make several copies of the pattern.

STEP 2. Adhere the pattern to the wood by spraying a quick-release adhesive onto the back of the pattern, not onto the wood. Let the adhesive set for a few seconds, then press the pattern onto the wood so its longest dimension runs with the wood grain (with-the-grain cuts result in stronger fretwork). Drill a starter hole in the center of each area you need to cut away, making the hole slightly larger than the saw blade.

STEP 3. Make outside and interior cuts, leaving the most delicate sawing for last to minimize the chance of breaking or miscutting the design. Start with a No. 5 or No. 6 blade. For tighter, more intricate work, switch to a finer blade. At the outset, run the saw at its lowest speed. Speed up later for long, complicated cuts. Feed the wood slowly and steadily into the blade. You can saw inside, outside, or directly on the pattern lines, but whichever you choose, do it consistently. When making each interior cut, switch off the saw's power, loosen the tension of the blade, unclamp its top, thread the blade through the starter hole, reclamp and adjust the tension of the blade, and cut the opening. Cut the pattern design four times to form a circle for tabletop.

STEP 4. Touch up mistakes. When a cut wanders from the pattern, you have to throw away the work and start over, but minor deviations—when you haven't cut away as much as you should have—can be touched up. Use the burred right side of the blade to remove irregularities.

STEP 5. Sand all edges and wipe clean. Paint the fretwork; let dry. Place on table and cover with glass.

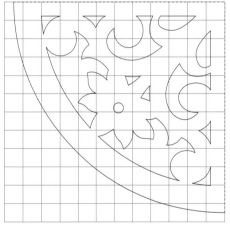

1 SQUARE = 1 INCH

# unusual tables

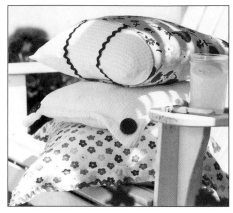

## 106 Getting Benched

**MATERIALS**

- Old benches and stools in varying sizes and similar shapes
- Wire brush (optional)
- Matte-finish water-base polyurethane (optional)

**START TO FINISH**

STEP 1. Collect old wash benches in sizes appropriate for your furniture. If the paint is old and flaking and you have small children and pets around, or if food will be placed on the benches, there is a danger of lead poisoning from the old flaking paint. Gently scrub the bench with a wire brush, and coat it with matte-finish polyurethane to seal the paint. (Although this will make the piece safer to use, it will likely decrease the value of an antique bench.)

STEP 2. For graphic impact, stack several benches together. A small bench placed on a larger one adds height to an arrangement. When tucked under a larger bench, a small bench can be slid out for use as a footstool.

## 111 Clothespin Craze

**MATERIALS**

- Old or new unfinished table with simple lines (the one shown is 26 inches high with a 12x17-inch top)
- White acrylic paint
- Round-top peg-style wooden clothespins (90–100 for the table shown)
- Paintbrush
- Drill with small bit
- Wood glue
- 1¼-inch (#17) brads

**START TO FINISH**

STEP 1. Paint the table and clothespins white. (Use the paint at full strength or dilute it with water.) Paint more clothespins than you anticipate using because some will split. Carefully inspect the clothespins before painting; some are likely to be damaged or misshapen. Let the paint dry.

STEP 2. Drill a small pilot hole through each clothespin at the same spot. The head of the clothespin should be just above the top of the table. Determine how many clothespins to use for each side of the table. You may need to leave a small space between each clothespin for them to come out even at the corners.

STEP 3. Place a dot of glue on the back of one clothespin, slip the brad through the hole, and pound it into the table edge. Repeat for the remaining clothespins.

## 112 Patio Pick-Me-Ups

**MATERIALS**

- Medium-weight solid-color and print fabrics
- Purchased square pillow forms
- Buttons or rickrack

**START TO FINISH**

**SLIPCOVER PILLOW**

STEP 1. From one solid-color fabric, cut two squares 1 inch larger than the pillow form. With right sides together, sew the squares together using a ½-inch seam allowance and leaving an opening for turning. Turn right side out and press to make a pillow cover. Insert the pillow form into the pillow cover, and slip-stitch the opening closed. (If desired, skip this step by starting with a purchased solid-color pillow.)

STEP 2. From a print fabric, cut a panel twice as long as the pillow cover plus 1 inch and two-thirds as wide as the pillow cover plus 1 inch. Press the long edges of the panel under ¼ inch twice to hem; topstitch. Fold the hemmed panel in half crosswise with the right side inside; sew the short ends together ½ inch from edge. Turn right side out. Slide the slipcover over the pillow.

STEP 3. Measure around a pillow end from one side edge of the slipcover to the other; add 1 inch. Cut rickrack pieces to that length.

STEP 4. Remove the slipcover from the pillow; sew the rickrack ends to the hemmed slipcover edges to make straps. Slide the slipcover over the pillow; loop the straps around the end.

# pretty pillows

### FLANGE PILLOW
STEP 1. From one fabric, cut two squares 5 inches larger than the pillow form. With right sides together, sew the squares together using a ½-inch seam allowance and leaving a large opening for turning. Turn right side out and press to make a pillow cover.

STEP 2. Sew around the perimeter of the pillow cover 2 inches from the edges, leaving an opening that matches the outer opening. Insert the pillow form into the pillow cover. Use a zipper foot to sew next to the pillow form, closing the inner opening and creating the flange. Slip-stitch the outer opening closed.

STEP 3. Sew buttons to the corners of the pillow cover or sew rickrack around the flange's outer edges.

### 113 Spring Greens
MATERIALS
- Terry hand towel
- Purchased contrasting-color pillow
- Two large buttons
- Ribbon

### START TO FINISH
STEP 1. Fold the hand towel in thirds so that one short edge overlaps the other by about 1 inch at the center of the towel. Sew together the open side edges to make a pillow sham. Sew around the perimeter of the pillow sham 2 inches from each edge to make the flange.

STEP 2. Center and sew a button on each edge of the pillow sham opening. Insert contrasting-color pillow into the pillow sham. Loop a length of ribbon around the buttons to hold the sham in place, letting some of the pillow show. Tie ribbon into a bow.

### 114 Rickrack Reunion
MATERIALS
- Cotton fabrics
- Purchased square pillow forms
- Jumbo, medium, and baby rickrack

### START TO FINISH
DIAGONAL-DESIGN PILLOW
STEP 1. From each of two different fabrics, cut a square 2 inches larger than the pillow form. Cut each square in half diagonally to make four triangles. Cut two pieces of jumbo rickrack 1 inch longer than the triangles' long edges.

STEP 2. Layer two contrasting triangles with right sides together and a piece of jumbo rickrack between the long edges; sew together the long edges. Repeat with remaining triangles and jumbo rickrack.

STEP 3. With right sides together, sew together the rickrack squares using a ½-inch seam allowance and leaving an opening for turning. Turn right side out and press to make a pillow cover. Insert the pillow form into the pillow cover, and slip-stitch the opening closed.

### RICKRACK-EDGE PILLOW
STEP 1. From the same fabric, cut two squares 1 inch larger than the pillow form. Cut four pieces of jumbo rickrack 1 inch longer than the squares.

STEP 2. Layer the squares with right sides together and a piece of rickrack between each pair of edges; sew together using a ½-inch seam allowance and leaving an opening for turning. Turn right side out and press to make a pillow cover. Insert the pillow form into the pillow cover, and slip-stitch the opening closed.

### DOUBLE-RICKRACK PILLOW
STEP 1. From the same fabric, cut two squares 1 inch larger than the pillow form. On the right side, sew a length of medium rickrack 3 inches from each edge of one square. Sew baby rickrack ½ inch from the medium rickrack lengths.

STEP 2. Layer the squares with right sides together; sew together using a ½-inch seam allowance and leaving an opening for turning. Turn right side out and press to make a pillow cover. Insert the pillow form into the pillow cover, and slip-stitch the opening closed.

### 115 A Mark Above
MATERIALS
- Monogrammed handkerchief
- Paper-backed fusible web
- Two 13-inch squares of white fabric
- Pressing cloth
- Purchased 12-inch square pillow form

### START TO FINISH
STEP 1. Trim handkerchief ½ inch beyond the edges of the monogram. Press the edges under ½ inch. Use the monogram as a pattern to cut a matching shape of fusible web. Fuse the web to the wrong side of the monogram according to the manufacturer's instructions. Remove the paper backing.

STEP 2. Center the monogram, web side down, on the right side of a white fabric square. Fuse the monogram to the fabric square, using a pressing cloth to protect the fabrics.

STEP 3. With right sides together, sew together the squares using a ½-inch seam allowance and leaving an opening for turning. Turn right side out; press to make a pillow cover. Insert the pillow form into the pillow cover and slip-stitch the opening closed.

## 116 All Dressed Up

### MATERIALS

- Six shirt fronts (for pillow front)
- ½ yard of 60-inch-wide striped shirting fabric (for back and flange)
- 12x18-inch pillow form

### START TO FINISH

NOTE: Use ½-inch seam allowances unless otherwise indicated.

STEP 1. Button shirt fronts together in unmatched pairs. Cut a 7x13-inch rectangle from each pair (see *below*). From the striped shirting fabric, cut a 13x19-inch rectangle for pillow back and enough 2-inch-wide strips to total 65 inches for flange.

STEP 2. For pillow front, sew one of the three 7x13-inch rectangles to each edge of the third rectangle. Sew short ends of the flange strips together.

STEP 3. Press the pieced strip in half lengthwise with wrong sides facing. Fold in ½ inch at one end of strip. Beginning at the bottom in the center with the folded end of the strip, pin the flange to the edges of the pillow front with the raw edges even. Trim the opposite end of the strip and fold ½ inch to meet at the center bottom. Baste the flange to the pillow front.

STEP 4. Sew pillow front and back together with right sides facing. Unbutton the pillow front and turn right side out. Insert the pillow form and button to close.

## 117 Grandma's Embroidery

### MATERIALS

- Vintage apron with a pocket, tea towel, and napkin
- Purchased square pillow forms
- Rickrack for apron-pocket pillow
- Vintage buttons for tea-towel and napkin pillows
- Muslin for napkin pillow

### START TO FINISH

#### APRON-POCKET PILLOW

STEP 1. Remove the pocket and any decorative trim from the apron. From the apron, cut two squares 1 inch larger than the pillow form. Sew trim or rickrack to the wrong side of the pocket edges. Center and pin the pocket, right side up, on the right side of a fabric square. Edgestitch along all pocket edges.

STEP 2. Layer the fabric squares with right sides together; sandwich trim or rickrack along the edges of the squares. Sew the squares together using a ½-inch seam allowance and leaving an opening for turning. Turn right side out and press to create a pillow cover. Insert the pillow form into the pillow cover, and slip-stitch the opening closed.

#### TEA-TOWEL PILLOW

STEP 1. Center a pillow form that is slightly narrower than the tea towel on the wrong side of the tea towel. Fold the towel in thirds so the decorative edge overlaps the plain edge at the center front of the pillow form. Pin the overlapped edges and side edges in place. Blindstitch the side edges together.

STEP 2. Evenly space vintage buttons along the decorative front edge; sew in place through both layers.

#### NAPKIN PILLOW

STEP 1. From muslin, cut a square the same size as the napkin. Press one edge of the muslin square under ¼ inch; topstitch in place. With right sides together, sew the muslin square to the napkin using a ½-inch seam allowance and leaving the topstitched edge open. Turn right side out and press to make a pillow cover. Insert a pillow form that is slightly smaller than the napkin into the pillow cover.

STEP 2. Evenly space vintage buttons along the topstitched edge; sew in place through both layers.

# pretty pillows

## 120 Four Square

### MATERIALS

#### APPLIQUÉ PILLOW

- ⅝ yard of fabric for the pillow cover
- Two colors of fabric scraps for appliqué
- Paper-backed, iron-on adhesive
- Appliqué stabilizer fabric
- 18-inch pillow form

#### SUEDE CHECKERBOARD PILLOW

- ⅓ yard each of two colors of synthetic suede for checkerboard
- ⅔ yard of synthetic suede for base material
- Rotary cutter with decorative blade or pinking shears
- 18-inch pillow form

### START TO FINISH

#### GENERAL INSTRUCTIONS

If it's necessary to precover your pillow, cut a pillow front and pillow back ½ inch larger on all sides than a purchased pillow form. Using ½-inch seam allowances and sewing with right sides together, sew around the outer edges, leaving an opening for turning. Trim the seam allowances and corners; turn the pillow cover to the right side. Insert pillow form and slip-stitch the opening closed.

#### APPLIQUÉ PILLOW

STEP 1. Fuse the adhesive to the appliqué fabrics according to manufacturer's instructions.
STEP 2. Draw and cut the following patterns: 3-inch circle for center and 3x6½-inch petal. Trace one center and eight petals onto appliqué fabrics; cut.
STEP 3. Center and evenly space the petals on the pillow front with tips touching. Fuse the petals in place. Pin appliqué stabilizer to the wrong side of the pillow front and machine-satin-stitch around the petals using a wide, tight zigzag stitch. Fuse and satin-stitch the circle in place. Finish pillow according to general instructions.

#### SUEDE CHECKERBOARD PILLOW

STEP 1. Cut two 10-inch squares of each checkerboard fabric. Join two contrasting squares, wrong sides facing; stitch. Trim seam allowance to ¼ inch with the decorative cutter. Make a second strip.
STEP 2. Join one long edge of strips, forming a checkerboard. Trim the seam allowance and outer edges with decorative cutter.
STEP 3. Cut two 22-inch squares from base material. Center the checkerboard on one square and baste in place. Join the two base pieces, wrong sides facing.
STEP 4. Topstitch over the basting line and ¼ inch from the outer edges, going through all layers and leaving an opening for inserting the pillow form. Insert the pillow form and topstitch the opening closed.

## 121 Simple as A-B-C

### MATERIALS

#### HIGH TIED (1)

- Two dinner napkins
- Purchased pillow the same size or slightly smaller than the napkins
- 4⅔ yards of ⅝-inch-wide double-face satin ribbon

#### GROMMET GATHERING (2)

- Two dinner napkins
- Purchased pillow the same size or slightly smaller than the napkins
- ½-inch grommets and grommet tool (plier or hammer type)
- Narrow cording
- Fray-check liquid or clear fabric glue

#### LACY EDGING (3)

- Two dinner napkins
- Purchased pillow the same size or slightly smaller than the napkins
- Narrow cording
- Clear fabric glue

#### BUTTONED UP (4)

- Two dinner napkins
- Cocktail napkin in a coordinating pattern
- Purchased pillow the same size or slightly smaller than the napkins
- Four matching buttons

### START TO FINISH

#### HIGH TIED (1)

Cut the ribbon into 7-inch lengths. Tack the ribbons to the napkins, placing them 2 inches from each corner and at the center of each side. Tie the napkins over the pillow.

# pretty pillows

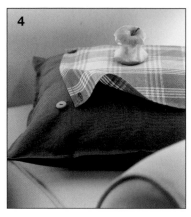

## GROMMET GATHERING (2)

Place a grommet 2 inches from each corner of each napkin, following the grommet tool instructions. Evenly space three more grommets on each side of each napkin. Sandwich the pillow between the napkins and lace the cording through the grommets. Tie the ends together. Treat the cording ends with fray-check liquid or dip them into fabric glue to prevent fraying.

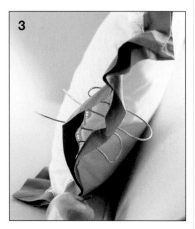

## LACY EDGING (3)

STEP 1. Dip one end of the cording in the fabric glue and let it dry. This will prevent fraying and make lacing easier.

STEP 2. Line up the holes in the napkins. Lace the cord through the holes at 1-inch intervals on three sides. Slip the pillow into the open edge. Continue lacing until the pillow is closed. Tie the cording ends together. Trim the ends and dip the remaining end in the glue.

NOTE: The band beyond the openwork will form a flange around the pillow. Because of the lacing, the edge may wave slightly.

## BUTTONED UP (4)

NOTE: You can eliminate the dinner napkins and the cover instructions by using a purchased plain-color pillow.

STEP 1. To make the cover, place the dinner napkins wrong sides together. Topstitch close to the edges of three sides. Slip the pillow into the opening and topstitch the remaining pillow side closed.

STEP 2. Make a buttonhole in each corner of the cocktail napkin. Center the napkin over the pillow and mark the placement of the buttonholes. Sew a button at each mark. Button the cocktail napkin over the pillow.

## pillow **pointers**

FOR A STREAMLINED LOOK, stack pillows vertically in graduated sizes. Start with a pair of large pillows; top with a pair of smaller ones. For example, pile standard pillows atop king-size pillows, or top standard pillows with boudoir pillows (12x16 inches). Finish each stack with a neck roll. This arrangement looks best using pillow shams with interesting edges and trimmings that reveal themselves in the layers. A monochromatic mix of solids, stripes, and textures works well.

IF YOUR DREAM BED is king-size and plumped with patterns, stand a trio of European pillows (26 inches square) behind a pair of king pillows. Place a standard pillow in the center and flank it with two small toss pillows. Stand a rectangular toss pillow in front. For smaller beds, remove one European pillow and reduce king pillows to queen- or standard-size. Mix patterns and colors to accentuate the size and scale differences. Needlepoint toss pillows, ruffled shams, and embroidered pillowcase edges look especially showy.

FOR A BED THAT'S A SNAP TO MAKE, try a casually tossed arrangement. Stand a pair of standard pillows in back, bridged by a European pillow turned point up. Top it with another pair of standard pillows and a boudoir pillow. Choose bedding that's loose and comfy in menswear stripes, plaids, and checks. If a pillow lands a bit out of place, who cares? This is casual!

# a way with walls

## 125 Plate It Up

**MATERIALS**

- Dinner plate
- Lightweight poster board
- Cutting mat
- Crafts knife
- Clear stencil acetate
- Interior latex paints in desired colors
- Stencil tape
- 2- to 2½-inch-wide paintbrush
- Small artist's brush

**START TO FINISH**

STEP 1. Make sure your wall is clean and free of film or grease. Use the pencil to trace the dinner plate on the poster board, positioning the plate so it is at least 3 inches from each edge (*photo 1*).

STEP 2. Place the poster board on a cutting mat, and cut out the circle with a crafts knife to create a stencil. Trim away the poster board around the stencil, leaving about 3 inches all around.

STEP 3. Cut a piece of clear stencil acetate larger than the circle but smaller than the piece of poster board.

STEP 4. Determine the placement of the circles by holding the stencil on the wall. Our circles are spaced 12–24 inches apart. Mark the center of each circle with a small piece of stencil tape. Label stencil tape with the paint color you want for that circle.

STEP 5. When satisfied with the arrangement, center the stencil over a labeled piece of stencil tape and secure it to the wall with stencil tape. Remove the stencil-tape label. Lay the acetate on a flat surface. Use the paintbrush to cover the acetate with paint (*photo 2*). Place the

painted side of the acetate over the stencil. Hold the acetate in place and rub around the edge of the circle with your index finger. Then use your palm and fist to rub the central portion of the circle (*photo 3*). Remove the acetate from the stencil; rinse the acetate in water.

STEP 6. Repeat for each circle, working with one color at a time to avoid having to clean the paintbrush after each stencil. Use the artist's brush to touch up any flaws.

## 127 Flower Power

**MATERIALS**

- Two colors of acrylic or latex paint
- Large and small sponge-style paint daubers (available at crafts, paint, and home improvement stores)
- Fine-tip marker
- Small scissors
- Paper plates

**START TO FINISH**

NOTE: Practice on a piece of poster board before painting the wall.

STEP 1. Draw a flower petal shape onto the flat surface of the large dauber as *above right*. Cut along the lines, then pull away the sections between the petals.

STEP 2. Lightly dip the flower-shape dauber in paint, then dab it onto a paper plate to remove excess paint. When most of the paint is removed, press the dauber to the wall to transfer the petal design. Reload the dauber as needed.

STEP 3. When the petals are dry, use the small dauber and a lighter shade of paint to create the flower centers.

## 128 Do the Polka

**MATERIALS**

- Two colors of acrylic or latex paint
- Large and small sponge-style paint daubers (available at crafts, paint, and home improvement stores)
- Fine-tip marker
- Small scissors
- Paper plates

**START TO FINISH**

NOTE: Practice on a piece of poster board before painting the wall.

STEP 1. Draw a scalloped center and edge design on one dauber. Snip along the lines and remove the sponge from that area, creating a ring shape that has a wavy edge, as *above*.

# a way with walls

STEP 2. Lightly dip the plain dauber in dark paint, then dab it onto a paper plate to remove excess paint. When most of the paint is removed, press the dauber to the wall to transfer the round design. Reload the dauber as needed.

STEP 3. When the dots are dry, use the ring-shape dauber and a lighter shade of paint and stamp over the dots to create the finished pattern.

## 130 Spice Is Nice

### MATERIALS

- Spice, herb, and other kitchen-style images
- Clear spray sealer
- Level
- Low-tack painter's tape
- Wallpaper paste or decoupage medium
- Striped wallpaper or wallpaper border
- Small-link decorative chain
- Decorative picture hook
- Two decorative tacks
- Ribbon for bow (optional)

### START TO FINISH

STEP 1. Make color photocopies of the images, enlarging or reducing for compatible sizes. Trim away the excess paper, then spray the

papers with sealer to protect them from moisture and soil.

STEP 2. Using a level, mark the placement of the images on the wall. Tape them in place and make any adjustments in placement and design. Adhere the prints to the wall with wallpaper paste or decoupage medium, smoothing out any air bubbles or excess glue with a soft rag and your fingers.

STEP 3. To emphasize the center image and create a focal point, frame it with strips of the wallpaper or border. If the wallpaper has a bow design, cut out the bow and adhere it to the wall, centering it several inches above the center print. If the wallpaper does not have a bow in the pattern, make a bow from ribbon and glue it to the wall. Place a decorative picture hook over the bow. Loop a piece of chain over the hook and to each upper corner of the center image. Tack the chain to the wall at these corners and trim away the excess chain to look as if the image is suspended from the chains.

STEP 4. To frame the design, cut four narrow wallpaper strips or border strips, and place a pair of strips on each side of the arrangement.

## 131 High Ambitions

### MATERIALS

- Botanical prints
- Picture frames
- Clear spray sealer
- Low-tack painter's tape
- Wallpaper paste or decoupage medium
- Level

### START TO FINISH

STEP 1. Photocopy the prints and frame in color, adjusting the sizes if necessary. Trim away

any excess paper, then spray the images with clear sealer to help protect the paper from moisture and soil.

STEP 2. Using a level, mark the placement of the images on the wall. Tack them in place with tape and make any necessary adjustments. Adhere the prints to the wall with wallpaper paste or decoupage medium, smoothing out any air bubbles or excess glue with a soft rag and your fingers. After the prints dry, glue the frames over the prints in the same manner.

## 132 Looking 'Tile-ish'

### MATERIALS

- Prints or other images that resemble tile
- Clear spray sealer
- Low-tack painter's tape
- Wallpaper paste or decoupage medium
- Mirror
- Clear clips for hanging the mirror
- Decorative braid
- Hot-glue gun and glue sticks
- Fray-check liquid

### START TO FINISH

STEP 1. Make color photocopies of the images so they are all the same size. Trim away the excess paper, then spray the papers with spray sealer to protect them from moisture and soil.

STEP 2. Using a level, mark the placement of the images on the wall. Work around existing fixtures, such as lights, and leave an opening for a mirror. Run a row of prints at chair-rail height, approximately 30 inches from the floor. Tack the prints in place with tape and make any necessary adjustments.

# a way with walls

STEP 3. Adhere the prints to the wall with wallpaper paste or decoupage medium, smoothing out any air bubbles or excess glue with a soft rag and your fingers.

STEP 4. Hang a mirror, cut to fit the opening between the "tiles," using clear mirror clips. Hot-glue braid to cover the edges of the prints. Treat cut edges of the braid with fray-check liquid.

## 134 Big-Time Results

MATERIALS

- Large prints or small posters with similar colors and themes
- Clear spray sealer
- Low-tack painter's tape
- Wallpaper paste or decoupage medium
- Level
- ¼-inch-wide grosgrain ribbon
- Decorative upholstery tacks

### START TO FINISH

STEP 1. Trim away any excess margin from the posters, then spray the images with clear sealer to help protect the paper from moisture and soil.

STEP 2. Using a level, mark the placement of the images on the wall. Tack them in place with tape and make any necessary adjustments. Adhere the prints to the wall with wallpaper paste or decoupage medium, smoothing out any air bubbles or excess glue with a soft rag and your fingers. If you place them over wallpaper, use special vinyl-to-vinyl wallpaper paste.

STEP 3. Run the ribbon around each print, tacking it at the corners. If necessary, tack it in place with glue to keep it from sagging.

## 138 All That Glitters

MATERIALS

- Poster board
- Crafts knife
- Spray polyurethane sealer
- Colored paper
- Stencil adhesive
- Level
- Metallic copper spray paint

### START TO FINISH

STEP 1. Make sure the wall is clean and free of film or grease. Cut a 3-inch square in the center of the poster board, making sure the edges of the square are parallel with the edges of the poster board. Seal the poster board with a coat of polyurethane.

STEP 2. Cut 2½-inch squares from paper. Tape them to the wall to determine the placement of the painted squares. When you are satisfied with the arrangement, spray the back of the poster board with stencil adhesive and position it over one paper square. Remove the paper. Use the level to make sure the poster board is straight. Seal the poster board to the wall and spray metallic paint through the square opening. Remove the poster board and repeat for the other squares. When the metallic paint is dry, place the poster board back over each painted square, aligning them perfectly. Seal the paint with a coat of polyurethane sealer.

## 139 Freehand

MATERIALS

- Metallic copper acrylic paint (choose a good artist's paint for maximum coverage)
- Narrow artist's brush with 1⅛-inch-long bristles
- Level

### START TO FINISH

STEP 1. Make sure the wall is clean and free of film or grease. Mark a beginning line from ceiling to chair rail, using a level to make sure it is straight. Mark the remaining lines at 6- and 9-inch intervals, checking to make sure they are straight. Mark a second line ¼ inch to the right of each original line.

STEP 2. Mix the paint with a few drops of water until it is the consistency of cream. Starting at the top and using even pressure, paint over the lines, as *below*. Stand under your brush so your hand is overhead. Look at the line ahead of the brush, watching the direction you will be painting instead of watching the brush. When the color starts to thin, reload the brush. The lines should be uneven and slightly wavy for a hand-painted look.

# a way with walls

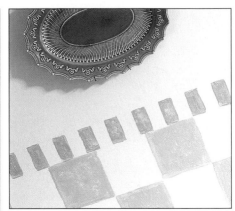

## 140 Stripe It Rich

**MATERIALS**

- Light green and dark green latex paints
- Copper-color textured paint (available in paint and home improvement stores)
- Paint roller and tray, plain roller covers, and ⅜-inch-nap roller cover
- Low-tack painter's tape
- Level

**START TO FINISH**

STEP 1. Paint the wall light green. After it dries, use a level to mark off the stripes. The room shown has stripes 6, 12, 18, and 30 inches wide, but you can use whatever widths you desire. Mask off the largest stripes, and paint them dark green. When dry, remove the tape.

STEP 2. Mask off the second- and third-largest stripes, and paint them copper, using a ⅜-inch-nap roller and following the manufacturer's directions. For best results, use one even coat from top to bottom when applying textured paint. When the paint dries, remove the tape. The smallest stripes will remain light green.

## 141 Check Things Out

**MATERIALS**

- Satin or semigloss latex interior paints in two colors (we used off-white and sage green)
- Paint roller and tray
- Carpenter's level
- Colored pencil in same color as checkerboard paint
- Clear decorator's glazing medium
- Paintbrush
- Sea sponge

**START TO FINISH**

STEP 1. Base-coat walls; let dry. Mark every 4 inches along the baseboard and up the walls to desired height. Using the carpenter's level and colored pencil, connect the marks, creating a checkerboard grid.

STEP 2. For a border of rectangles, as *above*, draw a line 2 inches above the checkerboard's top horizontal line. Draw vertical lines between the top horizontal lines every 1½ inches.

STEP 3. Mix 1 part of the second paint color with 4 parts glazing medium. Paint alternating squares and border rectangles a few at a time, outlining the shapes with the paintbrush, then using the sea sponge to fill them in. Let dry.

## 142 Friends Finale

**MATERIALS**

- Lightweight cardboard
- Low-tack painter's tape
- Oil-base paint in the desired colors plus off-white
- Oil-base glazing medium
- Turpentine or paint thinner
- Paintbrushes
- Paint roller
- Clean lint-free paint rags

**START TO FINISH**

STEP 1. Make sure the wall is clean and free of film or grease. Draw a diamond shape onto the cardboard; cut out. The size of the walls will determine the size of the diamonds. Lightly trace the diamonds onto the wall, spacing them randomly. Trace partial diamonds around windows and doors and along the ceiling and baseboards. Tape around the diamonds, sealing the tape to the wall with a piece of rigid plastic.

STEP 2. Mix each paint color with an equal part glazing medium and an equal part turpentine or paint thinner. Paint each square; let dry at least 12 hours.

STEP 3. Mix the off-white paint, glazing medium, and turpentine in the same manner as above. Roll mixture over the entire wall. Blot off most of the glaze with clean paint rags to create a soft, aged effect.

# a way with walls

## 143 Three's a Charm

MATERIALS

- Latex interior paints in two colors
- Paint rollers and trays
- Level
- Colored pencil in a color that will be visible on painted walls
- Low-tack painter's tape
- Clear decorator's glazing medium
- 4-inch linen paintbrush
- Ginkgo-leaf stencil
- Stencil adhesive
- Paper plate and paper towels
- Stencil brush
- Sponge
- Dishwashing detergent

START TO FINISH

STEP 1. Paint the walls (we used parsley green) with a roller; let dry. Measure the width of the focal-point wall. Divide this measurement by the number of stripes desired to determine the width of each stripe (our stripes are 24 inches wide). Use a level and colored pencil to mark the stripes on the wall. Mask off a stripe, and press tape edges firmly to the wall with a rigid plastic card.

STEP 2. Mix 1 part of the second paint color (we used light sage) with 4 parts glazing medium; adjust the amounts to achieve the desired color. Use a roller to paint a stripe (photo 1).

STEP 3. Working quickly, gently drag the linen paintbrush vertically through the wet glaze from the ceiling to the baseboard. Repeat until the entire stripe has vertical lines.

STEP 4. Starting at the top and working quickly, lightly drag the linen paintbrush horizontally over the vertical lines to make a faux-linen stripe (photo 2). Remove the tape. Repeat to make as many faux-linen stripes as desired. If necessary, touch up bleeding spots. Let dry.

STEP 5. Lightly mark locations for ginkgo leaves on the faux-linen stripes. Our leaves are sparse at the top and middle, then more concentrated toward the bottom so they look like they're falling naturally into a pile. Partial leaves going off the edges of the stripes also contribute to the natural look.

STEP 6. Stencil the leaves on each faux-linen stripe as marked. To stencil, spray the back of the stencil with stencil adhesive according to the manufacturer's directions. Press the stencil onto the wall. Pour some of the paint used for the base coat onto a paper plate. Dip the stencil brush into the paint, then blot it on a paper towel to remove excess paint. Pounce the stencil brush on the stencil to make a solid, flat-color leaf design (photo 3). Let dry.

STEP 7. Wash away any colored pencil lines with a sponge and dishwashing detergent. If necessary, touch up bleeding spots with the appropriate paint color.

## 144 Grid Works

MATERIALS

- Latex paints in white (optional) and in two closely related pale colors (about two shades apart on paint chip)
- Double paint roller (designed to hold two colors) and matching roller pan
- Level
- Lightweight cardboard
- Low-tack painter's tape

START TO FINISH

STEP 1. Make sure the wall is clean and free of film or grease. If the wall is not already white or a similar light color, paint it white and let dry.

STEP 2. Measure the wall height. Subtract 6 inches (3 for the top border and 3 for the bottom border). Divide the remaining measurement into an even number of squares. Subtract 3 inches from the length and width of the squares and cut a cardboard template to this size. (The squares shown are 20¼ inches.)

STEP 3. Using level, mask off the top and bottom 3 inches of the wall. Place the template against the bottom masked area and mark the

## a way with walls

top of the template, making a level line all the way across the wall. Mask off 3 inches above line. Repeat, working up toward the ceiling.

STEP 4. Mark and mask the vertical lines in the same manner. Seal all the tape to the wall with a rigid plastic card.

STEP 5. Apply the paints to the squares following the roller manufacturer's directions, as shown on *page 257*. Vary the direction of your strokes to avoid harsh lines and to softly blend the colors.

STEP 5. After the paint dries, remove the tape. If necessary, touch up any ragged edges.

## sponging**technique**

Sponging adds subtle effects to any room.

### MATERIALS
- Paints for base coat and sponging
- Natural sea sponge
- Newspapers for blotting
- Cardboard

### START TO FINISH

STEP 1. Paint the base coat; allow it to dry overnight.

STEP 2. Wet the sponge with water, wringing it out thoroughly. Pour a small amount of paint into a tray or pie tin. Dip the sponge into the paint and blot excess on newspaper. Cup the sponge in your hand and push lightly onto the surface.

STEP 3. Space the patches of color evenly, but change the position of the sponge for an irregular, mottled effect. Close, overlapping marks have the most subtle look; widely spaced sponging with little or no overlapping appears more casual. Try spaced first, then fill in.

STEP 4. In each corner, hold a piece of cardboard with one hand to protect the opposite corner from being oversponged. Use a small piece of sponge to work in the corners.

## 149 Center of Attention

### MATERIALS
- Embossed wallpaper
- Coordinating embossed border
- Wallpaper paste and tools
- Straightedge and tape measure
- Sandpaper
- Narrow decorative ceiling molding
- Paint and brush
- Finishing nails
- Wood filler

### START TO FINISH

STEP 1. Mark the diamond on the ceiling. Sand the interior of the diamond and wipe it clean so the surface is completely smooth. Measure the width of the border and mark this line inside the diamond line. Cut the wallpaper to fit this dimension.

STEP 2. Hang the wallpaper according to the manufacturer's directions. You may need to piece the paper for large diamonds.

STEP 3. Hang the border around the center diamond, mitering the corners. If desired, paint the wallpaper and border.

STEP 4. Cut the narrow molding to fit over the edge of the border. Paint the molding. Nail the molding to the ceiling over the border edge. Fill the holes and retouch the paint.

## 150 By Design

### MATERIALS
- Tape measure and straightedge
- Low-tack painter's tape
- Paints: base color, metallic glaze, border color
- Wallpaper brush
- Paintbrush

### START TO FINISH

STEP 1. Make sure your ceiling is clean, smooth, and free of blemishes and cracks. Draw three large equal squares onto the ceiling, positioning them on the diagonal, point-to-point. Mask off the outer 1½ inches of each square with painter's tape. Seal the tape to the ceiling with a rigid plastic card. Paint the base coat. When dry, add the metallic glaze. Run the wallpaper brush through the glaze to create a simple painted finish, as *below*.

STEP 2. After the glaze dries, mask off the 1½-inch border and paint it in a contrasting color.

# creative ceilings

### 151 A Perfect Tin

MATERIALS

- Embossed wallpaper
- Straightedge and ruler
- Wallpaper paste and tools
- Sandpaper
- Paint for ceiling (we used pearlized silver) and molding
- Paintbrush and roller
- Crown molding (we used lightweight plastic with a shelf top), chair rail, or other decorative molding
- Finishing nails
- Wood filler or caulk (for plastic molding)

START TO FINISH

STEP 1. Clean and sand the ceiling and upper 12 inches of the walls so the surfaces are completely smooth and clean. Following the manufacturer's directions, hang the wallpaper on the ceiling and the upper 12 inches of the walls.
STEP 2. Paint the wallpaper. Metallic or pearlized paint will give the impression of old unpainted or silver tiles, but any kind of paint may be used.
STEP 3. Cut the molding to fit around the room. Paint all the molding pieces as *below*. Hang the molding over the lower edge of the paper, nailing directly through the molding and into the wall. Fill the nail holes and retouch the paint.

### 152 High Marks

MATERIALS

- Three sizes of ceiling molding
- Paint in white and three closely related shades
- Paintbrush
- Tape measure
- Low-tack painter's tape
- Finishing nails

START TO FINISH

STEP 1. Cut the moldings to the proper sizes, mitering the corners. (Many lumberyards will do this for a nominal fee.) Keep the crown and middle molding square with the room, but the narrow inner molding can have an inverted notched corner added for interest. Paint the moldings.
STEP 2. Mark the molding placement on the ceilings. Mask off and paint between these lines, using closely related colors. Nail the molding over the ceiling, covering the lines where the paint colors change. Fill all the nail holes and retouch the paint.

### 158 Herbal Remedy

MATERIALS

- White acrylic paint
- Paintbrush
- Terra-cotta pots in three sizes
- Kraft paper
- Floral foam
- Sprigs of herbs

START TO FINISH

STEP 1. Dilute the white paint with water until it's the consistency of milk (see *below left*). Paint the pots with a light, uneven coat of the diluted paint for an aged effect. Let dry.
STEP 2. Place crumpled kraft paper in the bottom of the two bigger pots so the next pot sits at the right level when the pots are stacked. Fill the outer edges of each pot with floral foam. Insert herb sprigs into the floral foam, angling them outward (see *below right*) and filling in the center of the small pot. We used parsley in the bottom pot, sage in the middle pot, and rosemary in the top pot. Stack the pots.
STEP 3. Water herbs and floral foam frequently for several days of freshness, or let sprigs dry.

# outdoor looks indoors

## 159 Terra-Cotta Transformation

MATERIALS

- Latex gloves
- Large mixing container
- Portland cement
- Concrete bonding adhesive
- Stirring stick
- 1-inch paintbrush
- Leaves, flowers, or seedpods
- Terra-cotta pot
- Sponge
- Flat exterior latex paint
- Soft rag

START TO FINISH

STEP 1. Wearing latex gloves, mix 1 part water and 2 parts portland cement in a large mixing container (pour in the water first, then shake in the portland cement). Add 1 part concrete

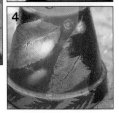

bonding adhesive; stir until mixed (*photo 1*).

STEP 2. Use the paintbrush to apply a light layer of the mixture to the ribbed side of a leaf, the face of a flower, or the head of a seedpod. Press the leaf, flower, or seedpod, mixture side down, onto a dry terra-cotta pot (*photo 2*).

STEP 3. Press the leaf against the pot with a damp sponge, wiping away concrete mix that seeps out. Let set for a few minutes so concrete adheres to the pot. Peel the leaf from the pot or pull up the flower or seedpod. Repeat as desired. (Leaves, flowers, and seedpods can be reused.)

STEP 4. Leaves can be silhouetted by holding a leaf against the pot and brushing concrete mix around the edges of the leaf to transfer the leaf shape to the pot (*photo 3*). Let the image dry five minutes. Remove the leaf.

STEP 5. Paint the pot with a color wash made of 4 ounces water, 4 ounces exterior latex paint, and 2 tablespoons bonding adhesive. Wait one minute after painting, then wipe the pot in a circular motion with a soft rag. As the pot dries, the painted concrete achieves a burnished patina, (*photo 4*).

## 161 Cascade Effect

MATERIALS

- 1x4 pine board to fit under the windowsill
- Purchased window box
- Paint: base color, metallic glaze, border color
- Paintbrush
- Sandpaper and tack cloth
- Screws

START TO FINISH

STEP 1. Paint the window box and pine board; let dry. Lightly sand the window box to smooth any raised grain. Wipe clean with a tack cloth, and apply a second coat of paint; let dry.

STEP 2. Center the board under the windowsill and locate studs to attach the board to the wall. Screw through the studs, placing the screws where they will be hidden by the window box.

STEP 3. From the inside of the box, screw the window box to the board in several places.

## 162 Points Well Taken

MATERIALS

- 1x4 pine boards
- 1x8 pine boards
- Wood glue
- Flat-head screws
- 1¼-inch finishing nails (3d)
- Metal shelf brackets
- Wood filler
- Paint and brush
- Construction adhesive (optional)

START TO FINISH

WINDOW BOX

STEP 1. Make the window box slightly longer than the window is wide. For simplicity, determine the size by planning out the box length in 3½-inch increments (the width of each picket).

STEP 2. Cut the front, bottom, and back from 1x8 as determined by the above measurement. Cut two 6½-inch-long 1x8 pieces for the sides. Rip the back shorter than the front to accommodate the window trim.

STEP 3. To assemble the box, glue and screw the front and back to the bottom, aligning the

# outdoor looks indoors

joined edge. Slide the side pieces into place, and glue and screw them to the front, back, and bottom.

STEP 4. From 1x4, cut the pickets 9½ inches long. To make the points, mark down 2 inches on each side of one short end. Mark the center of the short end (1¾ inches from each corner). Join the marks to form a point. Cut along the marks. Repeat for enough pickets for the front plus three pickets for each side. Rip the last picket to fit.

STEP 5. Glue and nail the pickets to the box. Fit the first picket on each side flush with the front of the box and work toward the back. For the front, start at one end and work toward the opposite end, aligning the bottom of the pickets with the bottom of the box. Countersink the nails, fill the holes, and paint the box.

STEP 6. Locate the studs below the window and mark the position of the lower edge of the window box. Screw the shelf brackets into the studs at this height. Set the window box in place and attach it to the brackets with screws. Paint the brackets to match the walls.

### PICKET WAINSCOTING

STEP 1. Measure the height of the pickets to align with the window box and to rest on the baseboard. (The pickets shown are 30 inches high.) Cut the pickets to length and angle the tops as described for the window box. Paint the pickets.

STEP 2. If the pickets will be placed around the room, start in the most prominent corner. For inside corners, cut a ¾x¾-inch spacer 2 inches shorter than the picket. Attach it to the wall with construction adhesive. For outside corners, rip the picket to fit flush with the corner. Overlap the cut edge with the picket on the adjoining wall.

STEP 3. Starting at the designated corner, glue and nail all the pickets in place so they rest on the baseboard. Countersink the nails, fill the holes, and retouch the paint.

## 163 Blooming Tales

### MATERIALS

- Ready-made window box (available at garden and crafts stores)
- Two or three decorative brackets, depending on the size of the window box
- Level and straightedge
- Screws
- Hardware for mounting brackets
- Paint and brush
- Sandpaper

### START TO FINISH

STEP 1. Paint the window box and brackets; let dry. Sand lightly to smooth any raised grain, then paint again.

STEP 2. Using the level and straightedge, mark where the bottom of the window box will fall. Mount the brackets to the wall so the tops of the brackets align with the bottom of the window box. Screw the brackets into studs or use anchor bolts. Make sure the brackets do not interfere with any structural supports on the underside of the window box.

STEP 3. Place the window box on the brackets. Screw through the window-box bottom and into the tops of the brackets.

## bedroom beauty lifts

## 164 Rescue Operation

### MATERIALS

- Vintage or reproduction architectural piece in scale with your bed
- Appropriate hardware for hanging (see below)

### START TO FINISH

STEP 1. Determine the point where you want to hang the architectural piece, making sure it is not at a height where you will hit your head against it. The hanging method will depend upon the structure and weight of the piece.

STEP 2. For lightweight pieces, attach several large picture brackets or picture rings and heavy-duty picture wire to the back of the architectural piece. Place anchor bolts into the wall, and hang the piece from this. For hollow-backed pieces, place long anchor bolts into the wall to extend the depth of the piece. Hang the piece over these bolts. For large or heavy pieces, screw a small strapping metal strip to the piece at several points. Screw the remaining end of the strip to the wall anchor bolts. Paint the exposed strapping strips and bolts to match the wall.

# bedroom beauty lifts

## 165 Garden Bed

**MATERIALS**

- Preassembled stockade fencing
- Sandpaper
- Latex primer and paint
- Drywall screws, anchor bolts, or other appropriate fasteners

**START TO FINISH**

STEP 1. Measure the width of your bed and the height you wish the headboard to reach. Purchase a preassembled stockade fencing panel and have the lumberyard cut it to size, or cut it yourself. Sand the surfaces and wipe them clean, then prime and paint them.

STEP 2. Attaching such a tall headboard to the bed frame may not give it enough stability. Using drywall screws, anchor bolts, or other appropriate fasteners, attach the headboard directly to the wall at several points on each side, then slide the bed up against the headboard.

## 167 Overnight Frame

**MATERIALS**

- Vintage or reproduction ceiling tins slightly larger than the bed
- Drill with bit suitable for metal
- Awl and hammer
- Small flat-head nails

**START TO FINISH**

Drill small holes on the outer edges of the ceiling tins. Hold the tins in place against the wall and mark through the holes onto the wall. Remove the tins and use an awl and hammer to make pilot holes at each mark. Replace the tins and nail them in place.

## 169 Fabric Frame-Up

**MATERIALS**

- Ready-made artist's canvas
- Decorator fabric
- Pinking shears
- Staple gun and staples
- Coordinating gimp or ribbon
- Fabric glue
- Nails

**START TO FINISH**

STEP 1. Determine the size of the artist's canvas needed to match up with the bed. Use pinking shears to cut the decorator fabric 3 inches larger on all sides than the artist's canvas, positioning the fabric to make the most of the design.

STEP 2. Spread out the fabric, wrong side up, on a flat surface. Center the the artist's canvas facedown on the fabric. Working from the back, staple the fabric in the center of each side. Finish stapling each side, working out from the center, as *above left*. The fabric should be taut but not distorted. Neatly fold the fabric at the corners to eliminate lumps.

STEP 3. Beginning at the center bottom of the artist's canvas, glue gimp or ribbon to the edges, as *above right*.

STEP 4. Position the headboard on the wall and hang from nails.

## 172 Flower Shower

**MATERIALS**

- 1x2 board, cut to shower curtain width
- Nails
- Floral shower curtain
- Ceramic drawer pulls

# bedroom beauty lifts

## START TO FINISH

NOTE: Before you begin, make sure the shower curtain grommets or holes will slip over the drawer pulls.

STEP 1. Starting ½ inch from the floor, measure and mark the shower curtain height on the wall. Nail the 1x2 board to the wall studs along the marks.

STEP 2. Measure the distance between the grommets or holes along the top edge of the shower curtain. Mark and screw drawer pulls into the board at those intervals. If you have a narrow bed, space the drawer pulls closer together for a gathered look. Hang the shower curtain over the drawer pulls, covering the board.

### 174 Upright Position

MATERIALS

- Curtain rod and brackets slightly longer than the width of the bed
- Purchased or handmade Euro-sham pillows
- 1-inch-wide ribbon or 2½-inch-wide fabric strips to coordinate with the pillows

START TO FINISH

STEP 1. If using fabric strips, sew them right sides together, using ¼-inch seam allowances and leaving the short ends open. Turn the strips to the right side.

STEP 2. Cut the ribbon or fabric strips to twice the depth of the pillow flange plus 1 inch. Turn the raw edges of the strips to the inside and sew the openings closed, or narrowly hem the ends of the ribbons. Sew the strips or ribbons into loops, overlapping the ends by 1 inch. Tack the loops to the pillow at the base of the flange.

STEP 3. Hold pillows to the wall to determine the height of the curtain rod. Hang the brackets according to the manufacturer's directions. Slide the pillows onto the rod, and lay the rod in place.

### 182 Arbor Day

MATERIALS

- Purchased arbor or arbor kit to fit around the bed
- 1x12 pine board
- Plywood
- 2x2 boards
- Wood glue
- Screws
- Wood filler
- Paint
- Batting and floral fabric (optional)

START TO FINISH

STEP 1. Assemble the arbor, if necessary, and then paint it.

STEP 2. To attach the arbor to the wall, cut a 2x2 cleat to fit between the arbor sides. Screw the cleat to the wall 24 inches from the floor, making sure it is level. Rip the 1x12 to 9 inches wide. Cut it the same length as the cleat. This will form the top of the shelf. Cut a front piece from plywood 18 inches deep by the length of the shelf top. Cut two 24-inch-long legs from the 2x2. Glue and screw the legs to the front piece, aligning the outer and top edges. Glue and screw the shelf top to the cleat. Slide the leg assembly under the shelf top, and glue and screw it into place.

STEP 3. Paint the shelf, or cover it with quilt batting and floral fabric. Screw the arbor to the frame. Fill any holes and retouch the paint.

### 183 Tubular Magic

MATERIALS

- Three 18-inch pieces of white PVC pipe
- Three threaded plugs to fit the pipe
- Three white metal flanges to fit the plugs
- Three caps for PVC pipe
- Three decorative wooden rosettes
- White paint
- Screws
- Glue for PVC pipe
- Two twin bed sheets in coordinating patterns

START TO FINISH

STEP 1. Mark a point over the center of the bed near the ceiling. Mark points on each side of the bed where you wish to position the side brackets. Screw a flange to the wall at each of the marked points.

STEP 2. Paint the rosettes white and, if necessary, paint the PVC pieces. Glue a threaded plug to one end of each pipe. Place a cap on the other end and glue a decorative wooden rosette to each cap. Screw the pipes into the metal flanges.

STEP 3. Measure from the floor over all three brackets and back to the floor for the length of the canopy panel. Cut each sheet into 19-inch-wide strips to equal the length measurement, piecing as necessary. With the right sides of the panels facing, sew them together using ½-inch seam allowances. Leave one short end open for turning. Turn the panel right side out, press under the open edges, and sew the opening closed. Drape the canopy panel over the brackets.

# fanciful floors

## 186 Tapestry Dance

### MATERIALS

- Tapestry fabric
- Solid-color upholstery fabric
- Yardstick
- Plate (optional)
- Fade-out fabric marker
- Iron-on adhesive, such as Wonder-Under brand

### START TO FINISH

STEP 1. Cut the tapestry to the desired rug size. Cut solid-color backing 2 inches wider and 2 inches longer than the tapestry piece.

STEP 2. Determine the desired width of your rug border and add 1 inch. On the wrong side of the solid-color fabric, use a yardstick and a fabric marker to measure and mark the border as desired. (Our border is 2 inches wide all the way around. We traced around a plate to create the curved corner design.) To create the fabric frame, cut on the drawn lines, discarding the center portion.

STEP 3. Using the solid-color fabric frame as a pattern, cut the iron-on adhesive to the same shape, piecing as necessary. Working on a firm ironing surface, fuse iron-on adhesive to frame, following manufacturer's directions. Peel away paper backing from adhesive.

STEP 4. Layer the pieces and fuse together, taking care not to fuse outside edges of frame.

STEP 5. To finish the rug, fold the outside edges of the frame to the wrong side; fuse in place.

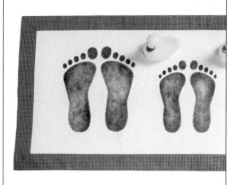

## 190 Family Footprints

### MATERIALS

- 20x50-inch piece of off-white canvas
- Stencil spray adhesive
- Stencil acetate
- Self-healing cutting mat
- Sharp crafts knife or stencil-cutting tool
- Sandpaper
- Paper towels
- Black acrylic fabric paint
- Plastic foam plate
- Stencil brush
- 28x60-inch piece of gingham fabric for backing and binding

### START TO FINISH

STEP 1. Wash and dry canvas to remove any sizing.

STEP 2. Enlarge feet patterns *below* to desired size using copier. (For each pair, make only one foot stencil following these steps; flip stencil over to paint other foot.)

STEP 3. Spray adhesive on the front of each enlarged foot pattern; place stencil acetate on top (adhesive will prevent shifting).

STEP 4. Over a cutting surface, use a crafts knife or stencil-cutting tool to carefully cut through the acetate and the photocopy. Remove paper from acetate; sand jagged acetate edges.

STEP 5. Determine placement of feet pairs, leaving a minimum of 3 inches between design area and canvas edge to allow for binding. Lay a pad of paper towels under canvas to absorb any paint that seeps through as you stencil. Work from left to right, keeping a clean sheet of paper under your hand to prevent smudging. Spray the back of a stencil with adhesive and position on canvas.

STEP 6. Pour a small amount of black paint on the plastic foam plate and dip the stencil brush into the paint; dab off most of the paint onto a paper towel. Use a pouncing motion to apply paint to the design area, building up color in layers and applying a little extra around the edges for a crisp line. Remove the stencil and let the paint dry. Clean the stencil thoroughly and flip it over to paint the other foot. Repeat for each pair. Follow the manufacturer's instructions for setting the paint.

STEP 7. Smooth out the gingham fabric on a flat surface, wrong side up. Center and pin the stenciled canvas, right side up, atop fabric.

STEP 8. To bind, fold backing fabric to the front so raw edges of the backing meet raw edges of the canvas. Fold backing to front again, enclosing the raw edges to create a border about 2 inches wide. Miter the corners; pin binding in place and press. Edgestitch binding. Blindstitch mitered edges of each corner together.

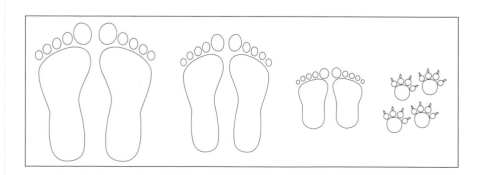

# fanciful floors

## wood-floor painting basics

Follow these instructions for preparing wood floors for the Sweetly Swedish and Paint by Numbers projects.

### MATERIALS
- Low-tack painter's tape (optional)
- Hammer
- Paintable wood filler
- Handheld sponge sander
- Medium- to fine-grit sandpaper
- Tack cloth
- Liquid floor cleaner
- High-quality flat latex paint
- Pad-style paint applicators
- Floor-quality, satin-finish polyurethane

### START TO FINISH
STEP 1. Remove old varnish or wax from the wood floor. If only a section of the floor is to be painted, tape it off with low-tack painter's tape. Remove any staples, and pound in all nails with a hammer. Fill gouges with wood filler. Sand the floor with a handheld sponge sander and medium-to fine-grit sandpaper. Wipe the floor with a tack cloth, then scrub it with a liquid floor cleaner. Let the wood dry completely.

STEP 2. Paint the floor with flat latex paint, using a pad-style applicator. For a flat, even look, apply two or three coats of paint, allowing paint to dry completely between coats. For a lighter, "pickled" look, use only one coat. Let dry.

STEP 3. After you paint your design and let it dry, use a clean pad-style applicator to apply a coat of polyurethane; let dry. Apply a second coat of polyurethane for high-traffic areas; let polyurethane dry.

## 191 Sweetly Swedish

### MATERIALS
- Flat latex paint in white and blue
- Paintbrush or roller and tray
- Stencil acetate
- Permanent fine-tip marker
- Piece of glass or self-healing mat
- Crafts knife
- Emery paper
- Transparent tape
- Lint-free cloth
- Paper towels
- Polyurethane

### START TO FINISH
STEP 1. Prepare and paint the floor white, referring to the Wood-Floor Painting Basics *left*. Let the paint dry.

STEP 2. Use a pencil to draw a large oval or circle on the floor where you want the garland. Enlarge the stencil pattern *right* to desired size, using a copy machine. Trace the design onto stencil acetate with a the fine-tip marker.

STEP 3. Tape the acetate to a piece of glass or a self-healing mat. Cut out the stencil on the traced lines with a crafts knife. Smooth any rough edges with emery paper. Tape over any stray cuts with transparent tape.

STEP 4. Align the stencil with the line drawn on the floor. Dampen the lint-free cloth with water and wring it dry. Dip the cloth into blue paint. Blot the cloth on paper towels to remove most of the paint. Gently press the cloth to the floor through the cutout areas of the stencil, as *above right,* dabbing on paint. Move the stencil to the next position, and apply paint as before. Continue in the same manner around the line to complete the oval or circle. Let dry.

STEP 5. Apply polyurethane following the instructions in Wood-Floor Painting Basics.

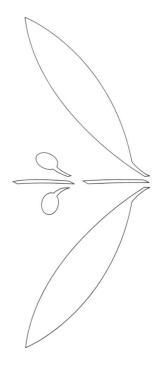

# fanciful floors

## 192 Checking In

**MATERIALS**

- Tape measure
- Straightedge
- Chalk line
- Low-tack painter's tape
- Utility knife
- Oil-base paint
- Mineral spirits
- Clean rags
- Polyurethane
- Roller with extension handle

**START TO FINISH**

STEP 1. Determine the size of the squares to suit the room size. Ours measure 23 inches across. Along the room's perimeter, use the tape measure, straightedge, and pencil to measure and mark where each diagonal row stops and starts. Use the marks to snap chalk lines on the floor, creating a grid.

STEP 2. Use the chalk lines as guides for taping the outside edges of alternating squares. Use a utility knife to cut the tape ends off straight. Press the tape edges firmly to the floor with a rigid plastic card, such as a credit card, so the paint can't bleed under.

STEP 3. Mix roughly equal parts of oil-base paint and mineral spirits if you want the wood

grain to show through, as *below left*. For a more opaque look, use less mineral spirits.

STEP 4. Use a clean rag to streak color onto the taped-off squares, creating a checkerboard. Allow the paint to dry completely. This could take several days, depending on the humidity.

STEP 5. Apply a coat of the polyurethane with a roller; let dry. Apply a second coat of polyurethane; let dry. If necessary, apply a third coat of polyurethane and let dry completely before walking on floor or moving furniture into the room.

## 193 Wooden Wonder

**MATERIALS**

- 4x8-foot sheets of commercial-grade plywood
- Ringed or mason nails
- Brown latex caulk
- Cloth
- Wood putty (optional)
- Hammer, screwdriver, or crowbar (optional)
- Permanent felt-tip black marker
- Yardstick
- Wood stain in cherry and walnut
- Turpentine
- Paintbrush
- Satin-finish polyurethane

**START TO FINISH**

STEP 1. Lay plywood sheets on the floor with the grain running in the same direction, or use existing plywood flooring. Use ringed or mason nails to secure plywood sheets. Fill gaps between the sheets with latex caulk. Wipe away excess caulk with a damp cloth. If you don't want nailheads to show, fill nail holes with caulk or wood putty. (We filled the holes with putty and later used a marker to draw fat nailheads.)

For an aged look, pound the plywood with a hammer, screwdriver, or crowbar.

STEP 2. Beginning at the center of the room, use the marker to draw parallel lines 6, 8, or 12 inches apart in the direction of the grain to simulate planks. Use a yardstick to keep the lines straight, but slightly imperfect lines are acceptable. The larger the room or the higher the ceiling, the wider the planks should be. If desired, incorporate all three widths. Draw perpendicular lines to establish the planks' lengths; these also can vary.

STEP 3. Combine cherry and walnut stain with turpentine. Brush the mixture on the floor. Let the stain mixture dry for 12 hours. Apply four coats of polyurethane, allowing each coat to dry thoroughly. Damp-mop the floor to clean it. Repair scratches by dabbing on extra stain.

## 194 Paint by Numbers

**MATERIALS**

- Flat latex paint in a light color and a darker bright color
- Large letter and number stencils
- Spray stencil adhesive or low-tack painter's tape
- Stencil brush
- Paper plate
- Polyurethane

**START TO FINISH**

STEP 1. Prepare and paint the floor in the light color, referring to the Wood-Floor Painting Basics on *page 265*. Let paint dry completely.

STEP 2. Secure stencils to floor with spray adhesive or tape. Dip the stencil brush into the bright-color paint. Pounce the brush onto a paper plate to remove most of the paint. Tap the

# fanciful floors

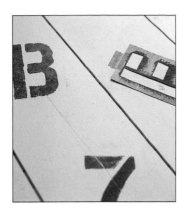

mostly dry brush onto the floor through the cutout areas of the stencils, as *above*.

STEP 3. When the paint is dry, apply polyurethane following the instructions in Wood-Floor Painting Basics.

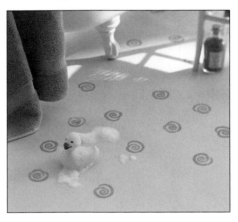

## 195 Curlicue Craze
### MATERIALS
- Liquid sanding solution
- Primer for vinyl surfaces
- Paintbrush or roller and tray
- Latex floor paint in two colors of your choice
- Plastic plate
- Deep-cut rubber stamp
- Wedge-shape foam sponge
- Water-base polyurethane

### START TO FINISH
STEP 1. Make sure the vinyl floor to be painted is clean and free of film and grease. Remove any wax from the floor. Apply a liquid sanding solution to roughen the vinyl surface so paint will adhere better. Apply a coat of primer to the floor; let dry.

STEP 2. Apply a coat of latex floor paint; let dry. If necessary, apply a second coat; let dry.

STEP 3. Pour a small amount of the second paint color onto a plastic plate. Dab the paint onto the rubber stamp with a foam sponge. Stamp the image onto the floor, spacing at random. When paint is completely dry, apply a coat of polyurethane; let dry. Apply a second coat of polyurethane; let dry.

## 197 A Step Above
### MATERIALS
- Tape measure
- Chalk
- Acrylic crafts paints in khaki, dark green, olive, light green, barn red, and white
- Paintbrushes: foam and round
- Paper (optional)
- Tracing paper (optional)
- Transfer paper (optional)
- Pencil or stylus (optional)
- Polyurethane

### START TO FINISH
STEP 1. Measure 5 inches in from the outer edge of the porch step; make a mark every few inches with chalk, then connect the marks to create a line that matches the curve of the step. On the riser, make a line 1½ inches from top of the step. Use the foam brush and khaki-color paint to paint the area between the two chalk lines, covering some areas lightly to create a mottled appearance.

STEP 2. Referring to the photograph *above,* use chalk to draw the design onto the step freehand. (Don't worry about perfection; draw

the design as a vine would flow naturally, with imperfections and in varying sizes.) Or, if desired, draw the design onto paper to create a template. Place tracing paper over the template, and trace. To transfer the design to the step, place transfer paper on the step, top with the tracing-paper pattern, and trace design with a pencil or stylus.

STEP 3. Using the round brush, paint the vine dark green. Paint the leaves olive. Use light green to highlight the leaves. Paint the berries and some leaf tips barn red. Add white highlights. Let dry.

STEP 4. To finish, apply a coat of polyurethane over entire design (including riser).

## 198 Set in Concrete
### MATERIALS
- Commercial concrete etcher
- Straightedge
- Silicon acrylic concrete stain in seafoam green, light buff, blue, and brick red
- Spray stencil adhesive
- Low-tack painter's tape
- Paint roller
- Graph paper (optional)
- Stencil acetate
- Permanent felt-tip marker
- Piece of glass or self-healing mat
- Crafts knife
- Emery paper
- Transparent tape
- Artist's and stencil brushes

# fanciful floors

**START TO FINISH**

STEP 1. Use the concrete etcher to acid-wash the surface, following the manufacturer's instructions and safety precautions. (Depending on the condition of the concrete, you may need to scrape and pressure-wash it before using the etcher.) Let the concrete dry for 72 hours. Concrete stain needs to dry 24 hours between applications, so the following steps are organized to decrease waiting time. When stenciling, use spray adhesive to keep the stencils in place while you work.

STEP 2. Determine where you want the "rug" on your concrete floor. Use a pencil and straightedge to outline rug. Use painter's tape to mask off the perimeter of the rug from the rest of the floor. Press the tape edges firmly to the concrete with a rigid plastic card so the stain can't bleed under. Measure in 6½ inches from the perimeter, and mask off the center of the rug. Use a roller to stain the center seafoam green. While this is drying, roll light buff stain over the floor outside the rug.

STEP 3. While the backgrounds are drying, enlarge the stencil designs *right* using graph paper or a copy machine.

STEP 4. Trace the designs onto stencil acetate with a felt-tip marker. Tape the acetate to a piece of glass or a self-healing mat. Cut out the stencils on the traced lines with a crafts knife. Smooth any rough edges with emery paper. Tape over any stray cuts with transparent tape.

STEP 5. When the floor stains are dry, remove the tape. Tape off a 5-inch-wide border around the green rug center. Stain the border blue. Let it dry; remove the tape. Repeat to add a thin brick red border around the outside of the rug.

STEP 6. Use a stencil brush and light buff stain to randomly stencil stars over the rug's seafoam green center, stenciling partial stars along the border edges. Use brick red stain to randomly stencil roses over the floor's light buff background, stenciling partial roses along the edges of the rug. Let dry.

STEP 7. Around each rose, stencil one to three leaves in seafoam green. Let dry. Use an artist's brush to paint a wavy line of seafoam green in the rug's blue border. Add light buff dots around wave.

STEP 8. Stencil the details in each rose using an artist's brush. To make the details look hand-painted, mix equal amounts of brick red

and light buff. Dip the brush in the mixture, then into light buff, being careful not to completely blend the colors. For some strokes, alternate colors. Remove stencil; make freehand strokes next to the details and randomly around the roses' perimeters. Let dry.

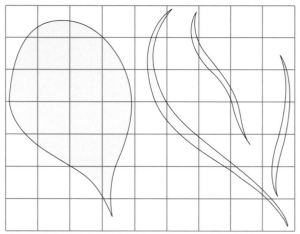

1 square = ½ inch

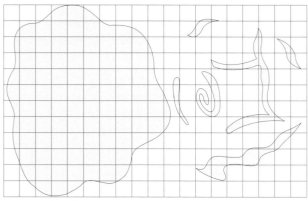

1 square = ½ inch

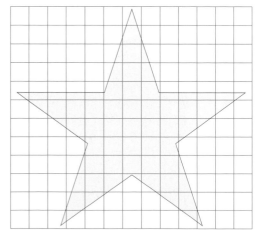

1 square = ½ inch

## fanciful floors

### 199 Follow the Brick Road

MATERIALS
- Commercial concrete etcher
- Straightedge
- Kitchen sponges
- Silicon acrylic concrete stain in brick red and light buff
- Paper towels
- Low-tack painter's tape
- Paint roller

START TO FINISH

STEP 1. Use the concrete etcher to acid-wash the surface, following the manufacturer's instructions and safety precautions. (Depending on the condition of the concrete, you may need to scrape and pressure-wash it before using the etcher.) Let the concrete dry for 72 hours.

STEP 2. Determine the desired border width and brick pattern. Measure and mark off the pattern on the concrete with a straightedge and pencil, leaving space between the faux bricks so the concrete imitates mortar.

STEP 3. Cut kitchen sponges to the desired brick sizes. Dip a sponge in the brick red stain, blotting off excess on a paper towel. Press the sponge within the pattern marks. Repeat until the pattern is complete. Let the stain dry 24 hours.

STEP 4. Lightly dip a brick-size sponge in light buff stain. Blot off excess on a paper towel so little color remains on the sponge. Press the sponge on each faux brick for highlights. Let dry 24 hours.

STEP 5. Use painter's tape to mask off a border around the faux-brick pattern. Press the tape edges firmly to the concrete with a rigid plastic card. Use a roller and brick red to stain the border. Let the border dry.

### 200 Squared Away

MATERIALS
- Tan latex paint (optional)
- Paint rollers and trays
- Carpenter's level
- White colored pencil
- Tape measure
- Low-tack painter's tape
- Acrylic paints in two colors (we used white and blue)
- Dinner plate or compass
- Frisket Film* or cardboard form
- Crafts knife
- Sponge
- Dishwashing detergent or shampoo

START TO FINISH

*NOTE: Frisket Film, available in crafts stores, is a vinyl film with an adhesive back. It cuts cleanly and is a quick way to make stencils.

STEP 1. Make sure your wall is clean and free of film or grease. If the wall is not already tan or

a similar light color, paint it and let dry. Use the level and white colored pencil to draw three equal squares on the wall, centering them over a mantel. Our 16-inch squares are 8 inches above the mantel and 2 inches apart.

STEP 2. Mask off the squares and press the tape firmly to the wall with a rigid plastic card to keep paint from bleeding. Paint the end squares white and the middle square blue (photo 1). Remove the tape. Let paint dry.

STEP 3. Draw a smaller square centered in each end square. (We used 14-inch squares to create 2-inch-wide borders.) Mask off the smaller squares and paint them blue (photo 2). Remove tape and let dry.

STEP 4. Use a dinner plate or compass to draw a circle on the Frisket Film or cardboard form. (Ours is 14 inches in diameter.) Cut out the circle with a crafts knife to create a stencil. Center the film stencil on the middle square with the adhesive side down and press. Or center the cardboard stencil in the middle square and trace. Paint the circle white and, if necessary, peel off the stencil (photo 3).

STEP 5. When the paint is completely dry, wash away any colored pencil lines with a sponge and dishwashing detergent or shampoo. If necessary, touch up bleeding spots with the appropriate paint colors.

### 203 Screen Gem

MATERIALS
- Fireplace screen frame
- Rag
- Paint thinner
- Spray primer
- Chrome-color spray paint
- 20- and 32-gauge wire

## fireplace focus

- Wire cutter
- Pliers
- Four sheets of tissue paper, each a different color
- Shallow bowl or pie tin
- Crafts glue

### START TO FINISH

STEP 1. Have an ironworks company make a frame, or remove the screen from an existing frame. (Our custom-made frame measures 30x38 inches and cost about $50.) In a well-ventilated area, clean the frame using a rag and paint thinner. Spray on the primer. When dry, spray the frame with chrome-color paint. Let the paint dry.

STEP 2. To begin the wire design, randomly string 20-gauge wire vertically and horizontally; with each length, wrap the wire ends around the frame, then coil the wire around itself. This will serve as the basic grid.

STEP 3. To finish the wire design, secure one end of a 20-gauge piece of wire to a spot on the frame, then loop it through the original grid in a swirling pattern. Use short lengths of 32-gauge wire to wrap the intersecting wires together.

STEP 4. Tear tissue paper into 1-inch-wide strips ranging from 1 to 5 inches in length.

STEP 5. Mix equal amounts of crafts glue and water in a shallow bowl or pie tin. Dip the strips of tissue paper in the mixture, then wrap the strips around sections formed by the wire loops and intersections. Layer different colors of tissue paper to create a stained-glass effect. Let the tissue paper dry.

WARNING: Do not set the fireplace screen in front of a fire. It is for decorative use only.

## 207 Letter Perfect

### MATERIALS

- Precut stencils: main alphabet motif and small geometric motif
- Liquid or creme stencil paint
- Stencil brush
- Stencil adhesive or painter's tape
- Paper plate
- Clear sealer

### START TO FINISH

Mark the center of each riser for the location of the small geometric motifs. Position the alphabet motifs on each side of the center mark. Hold a stencil in place with tape or adhesive. Load the stencil brush with paint, and tap it onto a paper plate until most of the paint is removed. Pounce the paint through the opening in the stencil. Carefully remove the stencil. Repeat to stencil motifs. Let the paint dry. Seal with clear sealer.

## 208 Brasslike Tactics

### MATERIALS

- Purchased runner
- Three or more shades of acrylic paint to complement runner
- Paintbrushes
- ½-inch-diameter wooden dowel for each stair
- ⅝-inch screw eyes
- Awl or drill with a small bit

### START TO FINISH

STEP 1. Paint each riser, alternating colors. (Because risers get very little wear, you can use small bottles of acrylic paint to save money and match colors.) Let dry. Two or more coats may be needed.

STEP 2. Cut the dowels 2 inches longer than the width of your runner and paint them to blend with the runner; let dry. Lay the rug in place, and place a dowel at the base of each riser. On the stairs, mark points ½ inch in from each end of the dowels. Remove the dowels. Make a pilot hole, then screw the screw eyes in place to hold the dowels. Slide the dowels into place.

# stair style

## 209 Up the Wallpaper

**MATERIALS**

- Two coordinating patterns of floral wallpaper
- Wallpaper paste and tools
- Black-and-white check self-adhesive vinyl paper
- Rotary cutter, mat, and ruler; or scissors

**START TO FINISH**

STEP 1. Cut and apply one pattern of wallpaper to the risers and to the outside wall of the stairway. Adhere the second pattern of wallpaper to the wall, cutting carefully around each step.

STEP 2. Using a rotary cutter or scissors, cut the self-adhesive vinyl into strips. Apply the strips directly under each step and along the edges of the wall pieces. The strips add a decorative border and also help seal the wallpaper to the wall.

## 210 Looking Up

**MATERIALS**

- White and blue latex paints
- Paintbrushes
- Natural sea sponge (available at crafts and paint supply stores)
- Paper plate or paper towels

**START TO FINISH**

Coat the risers with white paint. Tear off a fist-size piece of natural sea sponge. Wet the sponge with warm water, then wring it dry. Lightly dip the sponge into the blue paint, then tap it onto the paper towel or paper plate until most of the paint is removed. Gently dab the sponge on the stair risers, repeating until the color becomes faint. Load the sponge with more paint, and repeat the process to achieve the desired look.

## 212 Center of Attention

**MATERIALS**

- Paints for center, borders, and accents
- Purchased stencil, or stencil acetate and crafts knife
- Measuring tape
- Straightedge
- Low-tack painter's tape
- Paintbrush and stencil brush
- Polyurethane floor sealer

**START TO FINISH**

STEP 1. Mark the center point of each step. For the center band, measure and mark equal distances to each side of the center point. Mark a narrow border, then a wide border (about ¾ inch to 3 inches), on each side of the center band.

STEP 2. Mask off the center band using low-tack painter's tape. Paint this portion; let dry. Mask and paint the narrow and then the wide borders. Cut a heart shape from stencil acetate, or use a purchased stencil. Position the stencil and paint the motif; let dry.

STEP 3. Seal the stairs and risers with two coats of floor sealer, letting each coat dry.

# kitchen accents

## artistic tile

### 214 Make a 'Splash
MATERIALS

- Mesh-backed ¾-inch-square ceramic tiles in white, red, pink, medium green, and light green
- Graph paper
- Grease pencil
- Tile adhesive
- White grout
- Trowel, sponges, and other tile-setting tools

START TO FINISH

STEP 1. Chart the backsplash area on graph paper—one square equal to one tile. Repeat the rose pattern *below* in horizontal rows, alternating direction and position of the motif between rows.
STEP 2. Following the pattern, use a grease pencil on the mesh-backed white tiles to mark the placement of the colored tiles. Carefully remove the marked white tiles from the mesh backing. Apply tile adhesive to the wall following the manufacturer's directions. Press the mesh-backed white tiles into place. Referring to the pattern, press the colored tiles into the spaces, making sure they are straight and even. After the adhesive dries, apply grout according to the manufacturer's directions.

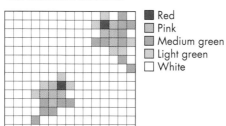

- ■ Red
- □ Pink
- ▨ Medium green
- ▨ Light green
- □ White

### 216 A Different Angle
MATERIALS

- Textural wood strips, such as lath, beaded board, siding, or barn wood
- Tissue paper
- Saw with miter capabilities
- Nails
- Sandpaper
- Tack cloth
- Clear satin-finish polyurethane

START TO FINISH

STEP 1. Tape tissue paper to the backsplash area. Draw the desired angle of the boards; mark the top and bottom lines to determine the angle of the top and bottom cuts. The laths shown are cut at a 60-degree angle, but you can vary your cuts to make the most of your wood. Cut out the boards according to your pattern.
STEP 2. Nail the strips in place. Lightly sand the strips and wipe them with a tack cloth. To make cleaning easier, apply two coats of polyurethane.

### 229 Hearth Warming
MATERIALS

- Several large floor tiles in black or another prominent color
- Floor tiles in taupe, white, and other neutral colors
- Old terry-cloth towels
- Hammer
- Tile adhesive
- Floor grout
- Tile sealer (optional)
- Trowel, sponges, and other tile-setting tools

START TO FINISH

STEP 1. Remove any existing tile or flooring from the hearth and clean the surface.
STEP 2. Break each large tile individually: Wrap it in a towel and hit it with a hammer. Uncover the tiles and reassemble them, leaving spaces between the breaks. Space the large tiles evenly along the hearth floor. Break remaining tiles in the same manner. Arrange them in a subtle, pleasing pattern. Remove the tiles, keeping them in the pattern as much as possible.
STEP 3. Apply tile adhesive according to the manufacturer's directions. Press the tiles in place. After the adhesive dries, grout the tiles according to the manufacturer's directions. If desired, seal the mosaic with tile sealer to keep the grout from staining and to make the floor easy to clean.

# artistic tile

### 231 Wall Nuts

**MATERIALS**

- Whole and broken tiles, plates, small flowerpots, snippets of screen, rocks, marbles, and other items
- Old terry-cloth towels
- Hammer
- Nails
- Mastic or other thick heavy-duty adhesive appropriate for walls and tiles
- Floor grout
- Sand
- Trowel, sponges, and other tile-setting tools
- Polyurethane

**START TO FINISH**

STEP 1. Leave some tiles whole, especially expensive ones. Break up the remaining tiles, flowerpots, plates, and other large items. To safely break the items, wrap them in towels and hit them with a hammer. Lay the items out on a table or floor to establish a design, rearranging and rebreaking any of the items as needed.

STEP 2. Apply mastic or similar adhesive to the wall and press the mosaic into place. For large or heavy tiles, support them with rows of nails until the mastic dries. Remove the nails and check to make sure all the pieces fit tight.

STEP 3. Mix floor grout and thin it slightly with water. Add sand for texture. Apply grout to wall according to the manufacturer's directions. After the grout dries, seal the mosaic with polyurethane.

### 232 Homemade Mosaic

**MATERIALS**

- Whole and broken plates, tiles, and other glass items
- Old terry towels
- Protective eyewear
- Work gloves
- Hammer
- Tile nipper
- Painted wood end table
- Masking tape
- Mastic or other thick, heavy-duty adhesive
- Spatula or latex gloves
- Grout
- Tile float
- Sponge
- Grout sealer

**START TO FINISH**

STEP 1. Break plates, tiles, and other glass items into small pieces. To safely break items, wear protective eyewear and work gloves, wrap items in towels, and hit them with a hammer.

STEP 2. Working on a table or the floor, lay out the pieces as desired, rearranging and rebreaking pieces as needed; cut pieces to size with a tile nipper. Arrange the pieces for the tabletop design, working from the outside edges in. To prevent a jagged or rough edge on the finished table, position pieces with the manufacturer's beveled edge around the perimeter of the design.

STEP 3. Put masking tape around the wood tabletop edge so the tape extends about ½ inch above the tabletop. Apply mastic or a similar adhesive to the tabletop, and press the mosaic pieces in place, leaving ¼- to ½-inch spaces between the pieces. Let the tabletop dry overnight.

STEP 4. Use a spatula or wear latex gloves to carefully spread grout over the surface of the mosaic tabletop. Press the grout into the spaces between pieces and gently scrape the excess grout off the top. Use a tile float to smooth and even out the grout. Allow the grouted tabletop to dry for several hours.

STEP 5. Carefully wipe away the hazy film on the surface of the pieces with a damp sponge. Let dry.

STEP 6. Seal the dry grout with grout sealer, following the manufacturer's instructions.

### 233 Shell Appeal

**MATERIALS**

- Terra-cotta pot
- White acrylic or latex paint
- Paintbrush
- Seashells
- Notched trowel
- Tile adhesive
- Gray grout
- Sponges

# just add paint

## artistic tile

### START TO FINISH

STEP 1. Paint the pot with a single coat of white paint.

STEP 2. Using the trowel, spread tile adhesive over a section of the pot (*photo 1*). Press the shells into the adhesive, either randomly or in a pattern of rows. Fit the shells as closely together as possible. Fill large, hollow shells with adhesive to help hold them better (*photo 2*).

STEP 3. Let the adhesive dry completely, checking to see that all the shells are tightly in place.

STEP 4. Spread and press grout between the shells with a damp sponge.

STEP 5. Wipe excess grout from the shells and pot with a clean, damp sponge (*photo 3*).

## 235 Spread Color

### MATERIALS

- Flat-finish white cotton duvet cover
- Two white European square pillow shams
- Standard white pillow sham
- FolkArt Acrylic paints: #459 Hauser Light Green (HG), #447 Leaf Green (LG), #901 Wicker White (WW), #635 Fuchsia (FU), #410 Lavender (LA), #918 Yellow Light (YL), #630 Poppy Red (PR), #961 Turquoise (TU)
- Textile medium
- Paintbrushes
- Hard-lead pencil
- Polyurethane
- Paper for template
- Kraft paper (optional)
- Low-tack painter's tape (optional)

### START TO FINISH

STEP 1. Wash and dry all the linens, then press them to remove wrinkles. Do not use any laundry products that contain fabric softener or stain repellent because they prevent paint from adhering.

STEP 2. Lay the duvet cover on the floor or a large work surface. Line with kraft paper to prevent the paint from bleeding through. Tape the edges to the floor or weight them with books so the duvet lays flat. Measure the duvet cover and divide it into squares, allowing about 2½ inches between squares. Make a template for the square. Draw squares onto duvet cover.

STEP 3. Make templates for three different leaf designs to fit within the squares. See the photograph *left* for ideas. Pencil in leaf patterns in random squares, leaving some squares blank.

STEP 4. For each color, mix paint and textile medium 2:1. (When combined with heat-setting, textile medium makes the paint permanent, even when you launder the linens.)

STEP 5. Lightly mark the color of each square FU, LA, YL, or PR. All solid boxes should be YL. Use the other colors randomly and make sure the same colors do not align. Paint each square, leaving ¼ inch of white around each leaf shape.

STEP 6. Pick one color for each leaf pattern. Paint the leaves HG, LG, and TU. Leave ¼ inch of white fabric showing between the leaf and the painted background.

STEP 7. For the bands between the squares, mix 1 part HG, 1 part WW, and 1 part textile medium. Thin with water if necessary. Paint the bands, leaving ¼ inch between the bands and the squares. Let all of the paint dry completely.

STEP 8. Using a narrow paintbrush, outline the squares and leaves with contrasting colors. Let the paint dry.

STEP 9. Modify the duvet designs to fit the shams. See the photograph *above left* for ideas. Paint the shams as you did the duvet cover.

STEP 10. Heat-set the paint using a dry iron on the highest setting and placing it on the fabric for 30 seconds. Set the entire cover and all shams. A commercial laundry can also do this by pressing the cover. To launder the linens, turn them inside out and wash in cool water with regular detergent. Dry on low temperature. Press if necessary.

# just add paint

## 236 Coming Up Roses

### MATERIALS

- Plain white fabric lamp shade
- Acrylic crafts paint in periwinkle, rose, yellow, and green
- Small containers
- #6 flat paintbrush
- #5 round paintbrush
- Spray water bottle
- Fine-tip permanent black marking pen

### START TO FINISH

STEP 1. Use a pencil to lightly draw rosebuds and leaves on the lamp shade, spacing them randomly. See *below* for reference.

STEP 2. For each color, mix equal parts paint and water in a small container. Use the flat brush to paint periwinkle and rose-color rosebuds, green leaves, and a green stripe around the top and bottom edges of the shade. Use the round brush to fill in the rosebud and leaf centers. To promote more bleeding of the colors, lightly mist the shade with water. Let dry.

STEP 3. Use the black marking pen to add details to the rosebuds and leaves.

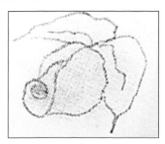

## 238 Sleep Ea-z-z-zy

### MATERIALS

- Pillowcases
- Shams
- Computer, printer, and paper (optional)
- Purchased stencils; or stencil acetate, cutting mat, and crafts knife.
- Masking tape
- Crafts paints
- Textile medium
- Stencil brush

### START TO FINISH

STEP 1. Select letters in desired fonts on a computer; enlarge and print. Or purchase stencils in various sizes. (Our letters, shown *below right,* range from 4½ to 13½ inches high.)

STEP 2. Place stencil acetate atop computer-generated letters on a cutting mat. Cut out the letters with a crafts knife (see *below left*).

STEP 3. Lay bedding on a large, flat surface with the right side up. Tape stencils randomly on top.

STEP 4. Mix 2 parts crafts paint with 1 part textile medium. Using a stencil brush, fill in the stencil letters using a small circular motion. Let dry; remove stencils. Heat-set according to instructions on textile medium.

## 239 Glassy Looking

### MATERIALS

- Assorted clean small glass bottles
- Delta PermEnamel Paints: Citrus Yellow 45005 (CY), Dark Goldenrod 45042 (DG), Eggplant 45045 (EP), Fuchsia 45013 (FU), Sea Foam Green 45027 (SG), True Green 45012 (TG), Ultra Black 45034 (UB), Ultra White 45029 (UW)
- Paintbrushes: Small round and small flat shaders
- Delta PermEnamel Clear Gloss Glaze
- Transfer paper (optional)
- Stylus (optional)

### START TO FINISH

GENERAL INSTRUCTIONS

STEP 1. Use bottles that are clean and free of fingerprints and soil. Use clean, dry brushes. Apply the base coats of paint and let the paint dry. Refer to the photographs to paint designs freehand; or use the patterns on page 276, enlarging them as needed and transferring them to bottles using transfer paper and a stylus. Unless stated otherwise, when mixing colors, load a bit of each color onto the same brush. Do not mix the paints together.

STEP 2. After the paint is dry, seal the bottles with clear gloss glaze. Follow the manufacturer's directions for drying, curing, and washing.

HOLLYHOCKS BOTTLE

Using a small, flat shader brush, base-coat the neck of the bottle FU. Base-coat the body EP. Paint alternating UB and SG stripes around the bottom edge. Mix UW and FU and use a round brush to dab on irregular spots of color for the hollyhocks. Mix TG, SG, and UW and dab on

# just add paint

spots of color to paint the leaves. Mix a small amount of TG and UB, and paint the flower stems. Using the tip of the brush handle dipped in UB, paint dots on the bottle.

## FAUX-LABEL FLORAL BOTTLE

Using a small flat brush, base-coat the lip of the bottle FU. Base-coat the neck of the bottle UW and the bottom of the neck TG. Base-coat the label area UW. Base-coat the remaining bottle EP. Paint vertical UB stripes around the neck of the bottle. Mix EP and FU with a small amount of UW and use a round brush to tap on dots of paint to resemble flowers on the label. Paint the leaves and stems TG. Outline the label with CY. Using the tip of a brush handle dipped in CY, paint dots on the EP area.

## YELLOW ROSES BOTTLE

Using a small flat shader brush, base-coat the lip of the bottle SG. Base-coat the neck of the bottle FU. Base-coat the upper rounded part of the bottle UW. Add a narrow EP band beneath the UW area. Paint the remaining areas of the bottle SG. Using a small round brush, paint UB dots over the FU neck area and then narrow vertical stripes over the UW area. Add TG stripes to the lip. Paint small CY swipes over the SG area to suggest small yellow roses. Let the paint dry. Add small DG accents to complete the roses. Paint leaves TG, and use the tip of the brush handle dipped in TG to paint the stems. Using the handle of the brush or the stylus, paint dots of UW around the roses.

## 241 Garden Art

### MATERIALS
- Framed glass
- Tape
- Clear self-adhesive vinyl shelf paper
- Crafts knife
- Latex gloves
- Glass etching cream
- Artist's brush or wedge-shape foam sponge

### START TO FINISH

STEP 1. Enlarge the watering can pattern *below* to desired size, using a copy machine. Wash the glass; dry it with lint-free paper towels or cloth.

STEP 2. Center and tape the pattern to the back of the glass with the image side of the paper against the glass (*photo 1*). Apply clear self-adhesive vinyl shelf paper to the front of the glass. Use a crafts knife to cut out the image from the shelf paper (*photo 2*).

STEP 3. Remove the pattern from the back of the glass. Carefully peel away cutout sections of the shelf paper, leaving a stencil on the glass.

STEP 4. Wearing latex gloves, apply the etching cream to the cutout areas of the stencil with an artist's brush or foam sponge (*photo 3*). Allow the cream to sit according to the manufacturer's instructions. Rinse with warm soapy water. Remove the stencil.

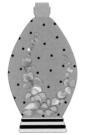

# just add paint

## 242 It's a Natural

**MATERIALS**

- Graph paper (optional)
- Clear stencil acetate
- Crafts knife
- Natural-fiber rug, such as bamboo or sisal
- Sheets of white paper
- Low-tack painter's tape
- Green acrylic paint
- Paper plate
- Stencil brush
- Paper towel
- Polyurethane

**START TO FINISH**

STEP 1. Enlarge the leaf pattern *below* to desired size, using graph paper or a copy machine. Lay stencil acetate over the pattern; trace the design with a pencil. Use the crafts knife to cut on the traced lines to create a stencil. (Make two stencils to avoid extra drying time.)

STEP 2. Lay the rug on a flat work surface. Determine your design by tracing the stencil onto sheets of paper or making copies on a copy machine and arranging the traced designs on the rug until you like the look.

STEP 3. Replace a traced design from the center of the rug with a stencil. Use painter's tape to adhere the stencil to the rug. Pour paint onto a paper plate. Dip stencil brush into paint, then blot it on a paper towel. Use a pouncing motion to apply paint to the stencil. Working from the rug center to the edges, repeat the stenciling process. When paint is dry, apply a coat of polyurethane.

## 244 Bedtime Story

**MATERIALS**

- Paper drop cloth
- Stencil acetate
- Crafts knife and scissors
- Low-tack painter's tape
- Spray stencil adhesive (optional)
- Acrylic or latex paints in French blue and white
- Textile medium for acrylic paint
- Stencil brushes
- Paintbrush
- Paper plates
- Ben linens
- Lightweight cardboard

**START TO FINISH**

STEP 1. Enlarge the headboard pattern *right*. Fold the paper drop cloth in half and transfer the pattern to the paper, placing the long straight line on the fold. Cut out the pattern, open it, and tape the pattern to the wall to outline the headboard position. Tape along the inner edges with low-tack painter's tape, following the curves. If necessary, trim the tape with a crafts knife.

STEP 2. Paint the wall within the outlines with two or more coats of French blue. Remove the paper and touch up any rough edges.

STEP 3. Enlarge the flower shape *below* to scale, and cut it from stencil acetate. To stencil the flowers, tape the stencil to the wall or seal it to the wall using spray adhesive. Dip the stencil brush in the paint, then tap it onto the paper plate to remove most of the paint. Pounce the brush through the opening of the stencil, creating a slightly uneven and aged effect. Using white, stencil a single flower onto the center of the headboard, as shown *left*.

STEP 4. To stencil linens, mix textile medium with acrylic paint following manufacturer's directions. Place a piece of cardboard under the area to be stenciled, and then tape the fabric tautly to your work surface. Stencil the linens in the same manner as stenciling the wall. If necessary, heat-set the paint according to the manufacturer's directions.

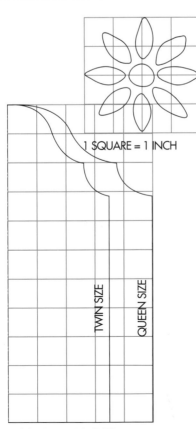

1 SQUARE = 1 INCH

TWIN SIZE

QUEEN SIZE

1 SQUARE = 6 INCHES

# the ottoman

### 249 Stylistic Overtones (First)

MATERIALS

- Purchased wooden tuffet
- 2-inch-thick foam to fit the tuffet top
- Quilt batting
- Muslin
- Staple gun and staples
- Decorator fabric
- Upholstery cord
- Fabric glue (optional)
- Fray-check liquid (optional)

START TO FINISH

STEP 1. Place the foam over the tuffet top, then cover it with batting and muslin, letting both drape over the sides several inches. Working from opposite sides, stretch the muslin tightly and staple it to the underside of the stool top 1 inch from the edge. Trim the excess muslin and batting to fit. Cover the muslin with the decorator fabric and staple it in place in the same manner.

STEP 2. To make the cover, measure from the floor across the top and back to the floor in each direction. Add 1½ inches for hems. Cut a fabric rectangle this size, slightly rounding the corners.

STEP 3. Try the cover on the stool and make adjustments. Turn under and press ¼ inch, then ½ inch along the fabric edge. Topstitch the hem, and cover the stool.

STEP 4. Cut cords to fit, allowing several inches to tie knots at the corners. Pin the cords in place at the base of the stool top, and tie a knot at each corner. Secure the knots with fabric glue or small stitches. Tack the cord to the cover in several spots. Trim the cord and dip the ends in clear-drying fabric glue or fray-check liquid.

### 249 Stylistic Overtones (Second)

MATERIALS

- Purchased wooden tuffet
- 2-inch-thick foam to fit the tuffet top
- Quilt batting
- Muslin
- Staple gun and staples
- Decorator fabrics for top and skirt
- Upholstery braid
- Hot-glue gun and glue sticks, or fabric glue
- Screw-type upholstery buttons

START TO FINISH

STEP 1. Place the foam over the tuffet top, then cover it with batting and muslin, letting both drape over the sides several inches. Working from opposite sides, stretch the muslin tightly and staple it to the underside of the stool top 1 inch from the edge. Trim the excess muslin and batting to fit. Cover the muslin with decorator fabric and staple it in place in the same manner.

STEP 2. Pin two rows of braid diagonally across the top, spacing them evenly. Add two more rows in the opposite direction. Glue the braid in place with fabric glue or hot-glue gun.

STEP 3. Cut the skirt fabric to twice the circumference of the stool top and double the desired depth. Join the short ends, right sides facing, to make the skirt. Fold the skirt in half lengthwise, right sides out. Press and baste around the top. Finger-pleat the skirt to fit the tuffet, pinning the pleats in place. The pleats can be slightly uneven. Staple the skirt in place. Glue braid over the edge of the pleats to cover the raw edges and staples.

STEP 4. Add a screw-type upholstery button at each braid intersection, slightly tufting the stool top.

### 249 Stylistic Overtones (Third)

MATERIALS

- Purchased wooden tuffet
- 2-inch-thick foam to fit the tuffet top
- Quilt batting
- Muslin
- Staple gun and staples
- Decorator fabric
- Fringe trim
- Upholstery braid
- Screw-type upholstery buttons
- Fabric glue, or hot-glue gun and glue sticks

START TO FINISH

STEP 1. Place the foam over the tuffet top, then cover it with batting and muslin. Working from opposite sides, stretch the muslin tightly and staple it to the underside of the stool top 1 inch from the edge. Trim the excess muslin and batting to fit. Cover the muslin with decorator fabric and staple it in place in the same manner.

STEP 2. Cut fringe trim to the perimeter of the stool top. Pin in place, then staple. Glue braid over the edge of fringe to cover staples.

STEP 3. Add screw-type upholstery buttons, slightly tufting the stool top.

# divide & decorate

### 251 Define Intervention

**MATERIALS**

- Purchased five-panel folding screen
- Tension rods for hanging the fabrics
- Two coordinating prints of light- to medium-weight decorator fabric
- Paint (optional)

**START TO FINISH**

STEP 1. If the screen has existing fabric panels, remove and discard them. If desired, paint the screen.

STEP 2. For the two flat panels, cut fabric 2 inches wider and 4 inches longer than the screen opening. Turn each long side under ½ inch, then another ½ inch, encasing the raw edges. Topstitch the hems in place. For the upper and lower rod casings, turn under ½ inch, then 1½ inches on each end; topstitch in place.

STEP 3. For the three gathered panels, cut fabric 4 inches longer than the screen opening. For the width, cut each panel two to three times the width of the opening plus 2 inches. (For heavy fabrics, double the width. For light fabrics, triple the width.) If the fabric has a prominent motif, such as the large floral medallion on the screen *above,* center the motif on the panel. Hem the panels and make the rod pockets as for the flat panels.

STEP 4. Slide tension rods through the rod pockets and place the fabric panels in the screen openings, alternating the patterns.

### 252 Make Adjustments

**MATERIALS**

- Three unfinished louvered panels in varying heights (ours are 6, 6½, and 7 feet tall, and 22 inches wide)
- Sandpaper and tack cloth
- Clear matte polyurethane
- Six double-acting hinges

**START TO FINISH**

NOTE: Double-acting hinges (also called swing-clear hinges) bend in both directions to fold either way and to fold screens flat for storage.

STEP 1. Sand the screens, and wipe them with a tack cloth. Apply a coat of polyurethane, as *below left.* While polyurethane dries, periodically move the louvers so they do not dry in one position. After the sealer dries, lightly sand the panels again to smooth any raised grain.

STEP 2. Position the panels with the tallest one in the center, using chairs or other items to hold them upright. Evenly space three double-acting hinges between each set of panels. Mark the position of the hinge holes.

STEP 3. Install the hinges according to the package directions (see *below right*). Make sure the bottoms of the panels align evenly.

### 254 A Trellis Nature

**MATERIALS**

- Four garden trellises
- Lightweight fabric
- 1½-inch-wide ribbon to coordinate with the fabric
- Staple gun and staples

**START TO FINISH**

STEP 1. To determine size of fabric panels, measure the screens and add 2 inches to the length and width. Cut a fabric panel for each screen.

STEP 2. For hems, press ½ inch to the right side of the fabric (right sides facing). Press under another ½ inch in the same manner, encasing the raw edges. This is the opposite of how most items are hemmed.

STEP 3. Place a panel on the back of a screen with right side facing the screen. Working from the back, place a staple in the center of each side of the panel. Working from the center out, staple the fabric to the screen. The fabric should be taut but not distorted. Repeat for the remaining screens.

STEP 4. Stand the screens, using chairs or other objects to keep them upright. Using ribbon, tie the screens together in pairs at three points. Keep the ribbon loose enough so the screens can fold and unfold but tight enough that the screens stay together. Trim the ribbon ends.

# divide & decorate

## 255 Three-peat

MATERIALS

- Three narrow hollow-core doors
- Four coordinating patterns of wallpaper
- Sandpaper
- Primer
- Wallpaper paste (unless the paper is prepasted)
- Vinyl-to-vinyl wallpaper adhesive
- Crafts knife, scissors, and straightedge
- Six double-acting hinges

START TO FINISH

NOTE: Double-acting hinges (also called swing-clear hinges) bend in both directions to fold either way and to fold screen flat for storage.

STEP 1. Sand and prime the doors. Sand them again to remove any raised grain.

STEP 2. The doors shown use four wallpapers: the dark paper (#1), the contrasting paper for the wide band at the top (#2), the narrow border applied as vertical stripes (#3), and the diamond-shape horizontal border (#4). Apply paper #1 to the lower five-sixths of the front, sides, and around to the back of each door, mitering the corners gift-wrap style. Apply the top #2 paper in the same way to cover the remainder of the doors.

STEP 3. If necessary, trim the border (#3) into stripes. Using vinyl-to-vinyl wallpaper adhesive, glue the stripes to the doors, spacing them evenly. End the stripes at the butt between the upper and lower patterns, as *above right,* and wrap them to the underside of the door.

STEP 4. If the remaining paper is not trimmed into an interesting shape at the bottom, use a crafts knife or scissors to create a zigzag,

scalloped, or other decorative edge as *above left.* Using vinyl-to-vinyl adhesive, wrap paper #4 around the door at the base of paper #2.

STEP 5. Cut paper #1 to fit the backs of the doors exactly. Glue the paper to the doors, covering all the raw ends that have been wrapped to the back.

STEP 6. Line up the doors and apply the hinges, following package instructions.

## 256 From Ho-Hum to Amazing

MATERIALS

- Fresh willow branches
- Pinecones
- Two wood-and-glass bifold doors
- Dark brown latex paint
- Paintbrush
- Garden clippers
- Hot-glue gun and glue sticks
- Power nailer or hammer, and 1¼-inch brads
- 1¼-inch brown ribbed panel nails

START TO FINISH

STEP 1. Gather pinecones and fresh, pliable willow branches from your yard or a riverbank. The branches should be 1 inch in diameter at their widest point. Scrape off bumps to smooth the wood; use willow within one week. If the two doors are joined, disconnect them; remove glass. Paint both sides of doors dark brown, as the willow will shrink and allow

some of the surface to show through.

STEP 2. Using clippers, cut three willow branches for each long side of each door, (*photo 1*). Position branches side by side, alternating the thickest parts from top to bottom so they will fit snugly; nail every 6 inches. Cut a branch to fit along the top of each door between the vertical pieces. Nail in place. Repeat for bottom.

STEP 3. Outline each arch by bending a length of willow; cut to fit (*photo 2*). Nail at its center, then at ends. Repeat on the back of the doors to create two arch rows. Outline side and bottom rims of window openings the same way.

STEP 4. For each door, nail four or five branches horizontally along the bottom. Nail a branch horizontally a few inches below window opening to create a narrow rectangle and a square. Measure a branch to run diagonally in the square. Cut the ends at 45-degree angles, shaping points to fit into corners. Nail in place. Make the other diagonal by cutting two short pieces, each with a pointed end to fit into corners. Nail in place. Fill in the triangles with twigs, starting at the center, cutting ends to fit, and turning the direction of the twigs (*photo 3*).

STEP 5. Halve the pinecones to create flat gluing surfaces. Hot-glue pinecones (tops and bottoms) to fill in the doors' rectangular openings and arched openings.

STEP 6. To create "windowpanes," cut and nail muntin pieces horizontally, spacing them as desired; nail one long vertical piece over these horizontals (*photo 4*).

STEP 7. For the door pull, cut a 5-inch length of a 1-inch-diameter willow, cutting a 45-degree angle at each end. Nail in place. Rejoin finished doors, adding a third hinge if needed for stability.

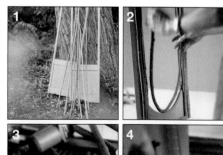

# kids' corner

## 268 Lovely Lullaby

**MATERIALS**

- Wicker basket (ours is 31x18x18 inches) deep and sturdy enough to support the infant's weight and movement; avoid rough edges
- Dense foam
- 3 yards gingham fabric
- 3 yards jumbo rickrack
- 18 yards ⅜-inch-wide twill tape
- 4 yards 1-inch-wide twill tape
- 1½ yards floral fabric for mattress cover
- 3 yards ½-inch-wide elastic
- Water-soluble marker
- String

**START TO FINISH**

STEP 1. Measure the basket; cut foam to fill within 10 inches of the top. Multiply basket height by 4, then add the basket length. For first runner, cut a fabric rectangle of this length and as wide as the basket. (Measurement includes hem allowances.)

STEP 2. For second runner, multiply basket height by 4, then add the basket width. Cut a fabric rectangle of this length and as wide as the basket is long.

STEP 3. Press under ½ inch twice on short ends of each runner for hems; stitch in place. Cut four pieces of rickrack to fit across short ends of runners; topstitch each piece to runner 1½ inches from edge.

STEP 4. Draw a wavy line above rickrack using water-soluble marker. Measure the wavy line with a piece of string. Cut a piece of ⅜-inch-wide twill tape three times longer than the string; sew tape to runners, adding a pleat every fourth stitch by tucking tape under presser foot with a pin (photo 1).

STEP 5. Draw two handle openings on the wrong side of the longer runner. To line each opening, cut a fabric rectangle the size of the opening, adding 2 inches to all sides; zigzag-stitch raw edges. Sew linings to marked openings with right sides facing. Cut out openings; clip corners, (photo 2). Turn linings; press. Topstitch around opening.

STEP 6. On long edges of runners, press under ½ inch twice. Place runners inside basket, (photo 3). Cut 1-inch twill tape into eight 18-inch lengths for ties; pin ties inside hems, positioning as shown. Remove runners from basket. Sew hems, catching ties in stitching. Tie the runners in place, so the liner will not accidentally cover your child and inhibit breathing.

STEP 7. Fill basket with foam layers. Cover 3-inch-thick foam "mattress" with a ready-made crib cover or make one. For mattress cover, cut fabric to size of mattress, adding 6 inches to all sides. Cut a 5-inch square in each corner. Join cut edges at corners, right sides facing; sew with a ½-inch seam. Sew a ⅝-inch-casing around raw edge. Insert elastic, joining ends so cover fits mattress.

## 271 Top It Off

**MATERIALS**

- Chenille fabric for valance
- Contrasting cotton fabric for valance border
- Assorted cotton fabric scraps for tabs
- Large buttons

**START TO FINISH**

STEP 1. Measure the window. Cut a chenille rectangle that is 1½ times the window's width and at least one-quarter its depth.

STEP 2. Cut a cotton strip that is 4½ inches wide and as long as the chenille rectangle. Aligning long edges, layer the right side of the cotton strip facing the wrong side of the chenille rectangle; sew together using a ¼-inch seam allowance. Press the seam allowance toward the cotton strip. Press the strip's long raw edge under ¼ inch. With the wrong side inside, fold the strip in half lengthwise so the folded edge covers the seam. Edgestitch the pressed edge. Press each side edge under ½ inch twice for hems; topstitch to make the valance.

STEP 3. Determine the desired number of 2-inch-wide tabs spaced 6 inches apart. For each tab, cut a 4½x10½-inch strip from one of the assorted cotton scraps. Fold each strip in half lengthwise with the right sides inside. Using a ¼-inch seam allowance, sew long edges together to form a tube. Press seam allowances open, centering seam on tube.

STEP 4. Use a pencil to lightly mark a point on each seam ¼ inch from the bottom edge; mark a point on each fold 1¼ inches from the bottom edge. Sew each tube from one fold mark to the seam mark, then to the opposite fold mark, forming pointed tabs. Trim seam allowances to ¼ inch. Turn tabs right side out and press.

STEP 5. Press the top edge of the valance under 1 inch twice for a hem. Slip the unfinished tab ends underneath the top hem, evenly spacing the tabs. Pin tabs in place. Edgestitch top and bottom edges of the top hem, securing tabs in the stitching. Fold tabs in half so pointed ends evenly overlap the valance. Sew each point to the valance with a button.

## 276 Study Hall

**MATERIALS**

- Desk or table with straight lines
- Cotton fabric
- Staple gun and staples
- Glass top (optional)

**START TO FINISH**

STEP 1. If possible, remove the legs from the desk or table. Or, if purchasing an unassembled desk or table for this project, wait to assemble it until after the pieces are upholstered.

STEP 2. Measure the width and length of the top, including the edges and underside. Add a couple of inches to each measurement for turning and stapling. Use these measurements to cut a fabric piece. If your fabric has a large motif, plan the placement before cutting.

STEP 3. Center the fabric on the top of the desk or table. Working from opposite sides and beginning at the center, staple the fabric to the underside of the tabletop, as close to the base

as possible and allowing any excess fabric to extend onto the base. Neatly fold the fabric at the corners; staple in place.

STEP 4. Measure the length and circumference of the legs; add a couple of inches to each measurement for turning and stapling. Use these measurements to cut a fabric rectangle for each leg. For added interest, cut on the bias if appropriate for the fabric pattern. Press a long edge of each rectangle under ½ inch. Wrap a fabric rectangle around a leg with even amounts at the top and bottom. Lap the pressed edge over the raw edge; staple in place beginning at the top of the leg. Fold under the fabric at the bottom so it just covers the leg; staple in place. Repeat with remaining legs.

STEP 5. Measure the width and perimeter of the base. Add several inches to the width, and cut enough fabric strips to more than equal the perimeter. Press a long edge of each strip under ½ inch. Staple the pressed edges along the top edge of the base, covering the excess desk- or tabletop fabric. Fold the extra fabric around the bottom edge of the base and staple it to the inside. If desired to protect the fabric, add a glass top cut to size.

---

## rooms that grow

Here's how to decorate rooms that change with your children:

INVEST IN A GOOD FOUNDATION. Choose well-made beds and dressers that will last, and high-quality carpet in colors that will endure changing schemes.

REFLECT A CHILD'S AGE and personality in things that are easy and inexpensive to update. Instead of a toddler-size armoire, purchase a full-size armoire, changing its paint and knobs as interests change. Similarly, patterned bedcovers are a cinch to swap for something more hip. Other easy-to-change items include:

- Lamp shades
- Wall color
- Wall accessories
- Window treatments
- Window hardware: rods, finials, and tiebacks
- Area rugs
- Storage bins and baskets

LOOK FOR LASTING STYLE and character in furniture. Sleek, boxy furniture may never go out of style, but you may tire of it. Consider antiques and primitives for a child's room, but be sure they meet current safety standards (cribs in particular). Search for dressers, bookcases, and other pieces that lend themselves to repainting.

# bath splash

## 278 Trendy Transfers

### MATERIALS

- Fabric
- Images from magazines, catalogs, or calendars
- Iron-on transfer paper (or access to a copy center)

### START TO FINISH

STEP 1. Prewash fabric. Transfers work well on flat-weave cottons and most other fabrics, but experiment on a swatch before using expensive fabrics such as velvet and silk.

STEP 2. At a copy center, color-copy images onto iron-on transfer paper; most copy centers will have it, but it's also available at crafts stores for use with ink-jet printers. Transfer paper comes in 11x17-inch sheets, so fit as many images as you can on each sheet. If your original picture is small, experiment first on a black-and-white copier to see how much it needs to be enlarged—this will save you costly mistakes at the color copier. To make black words, such as the ones along the bottom of this shower curtain, use a computer to enlarge the words in different fonts. Either print them on transfer paper, or print them on typing paper and take them to a copy shop.

STEP 3. Cut out transfer-paper images and words along their perimeter (*photo 1*). If your fabric is a color other than white, cut away the white background areas as well.

STEP 4. Position the cutout images facedown on fabric; iron according to the transfer-paper instructions (*photo 2*). Remove backing.

STEP 5. Toss image-transfer projects in the washer and dryer according to the fabric's laundering instructions; avoid drying on high heat, as the images can melt.

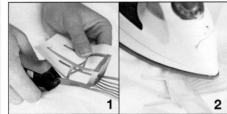

## 284 Custom Cabinetry

### MATERIALS

- Cabinet
- Wood filler
- Sandpaper and tack cloth
- Heavy-duty cleaner, such as TSP
- Primer
- Paint, paintbrush, and roller
- Knobs for drawers
- Flannel sheet
- Eyelets and eyelet tool
- Heavy picture-hanging wire
- Eye screws

### START TO FINISH

STEP 1. Remove the doors and hinges from the cabinet box and the handles from the drawers. Fill holes left by the hinges with wood filler. Sand rough spots on the cabinet box and the drawer fronts. Scrub the cabinet with a heavy-duty cleaner to remove residue. Apply a primer to all surfaces that will be painted. Paint the cabinet box (we used gray paint), including the inside, and the drawer fronts. Let paint dry.

STEP 2. Lightly sand the cabinet box and drawer fronts. Wipe the surfaces clean with a tack cloth, and apply a second coat of paint; let dry. Install knobs on the drawers (we used vintage glass knobs).

STEP 3. For each cabinet curtain, measure the height of the opening and add 4 inches for hems. Measure the width of the opening and multiply by 1½. Transfer these measurements to the flannel sheet; cut out. Press all edges under 1 inch twice; sew close to the inner pressed edges.

STEP 4. Evenly space eyelets along the top edge of the curtain using the eyelet tool. Thread picture-hanging wire through the eyelets. Screw eye screws into the side edges of the cabinet opening, and attach the picture-hanging wire to the eye screws.

STEP 5. For towel embellishment, from the leftover flannel sheet used for the curtain, cut a strip 1 inch longer and wider than the woven strip on the towel. Press all edges of the strip under ½ inch. Pin the strip to the towel; sew along all edges.

## 285 Savvy Sink

### MATERIALS

- Painted enamelware bowl large enough to fit sink opening
- Blue masking tape
- Power drill with a 1¾-inch-diameter metal-cutting hole saw
- File
- Plumber's putty
- Standard drain fittings
- Caulk (optional)

# bath splash

## START TO FINISH

STEP 1. Match the enamelware bowl to the countertop's precut sink opening. Determine the location for the drain hole in the bowl.

STEP 2. Cover the location of the drain hole with blue masking tape to help prevent paint from chipping from the bowl while drilling. Mark the center of the hole.

STEP 3. Remove the bowl from the countertop, and use the power drill and metal-cutting hole saw to make a 1¾-inch-diameter opening. Use a file to remove any rough spots from the edges of the opening in the bowl.

STEP 4. Place the bowl back in the countertop opening. Apply a bead of plumber's putty around the opening and install the drain piece following the manufacturer's instructions. If necessary, apply caulk between the bowl and countertop.

## 286 Earning Their Stripes
MATERIALS
- Solid-color towel
- Cotton fabric for ribbon base
- Pieces of washable ribbon in a variety of widths and colors

## START TO FINISH

STEP 1. Measure the width of the towel, and add 1 inch. Measure the depth of the towel's woven band, and add 1 inch. If the towel doesn't have a woven band, determine the desired height for the ribbon band and add 1 inch.

STEP 2. Use these measurements to cut a piece of cotton fabric for the ribbon base. (To embellish more than one towel, multiply the height of the base fabric by the number of towels. Use this new height to cut a single base fabric.)

STEP 3. Arrange a variety of ribbon pieces side by side on the base fabric, overlapping their internal edges slightly and covering the fabric completely. Sew the ribbons to the base fabric along the base fabric's long edges. (For more than one towel, sew at desired intervals and cut the ribbon-covered base fabric to fit each towel, allowing hems.)

STEP 4. Press all edges of the ribbon band under ½ inch. Position the band on the towel. Sew along all edges of the ribbon band.

## 287 Skirt the Issue
MATERIALS
- Fabric that drapes well, such as decorator upholstery fabric
- Light- to medium-weight drapery lining fabric
- ¼-inch-diameter welt
- Monofilament
- T pins
- Fastening tape with adhesive side and sewable side, such as Velcro brand Half & Half

## START TO FINISH

STEP 1. Measure the sink perimeter, subtracting the width of the plumbing in back. Multiply the perimeter measurement by 2½; add ½-inch seam allowances for each side. Measure from the floor to the bottom of the sink, adding ½-inch hem and seam allowances. Use these measurements to cut a piece of fabric for the skirt; if necessary, sew fabric pieces together to obtain the width. Repeat for lining.

STEP 2. With right sides together and raw edges aligned, sew welt to skirt fabric's bottom edge. With right sides together and welt sandwiched between layers, sew the lining to the skirt fabric along the bottom and both sides, leaving top edge open. Turn skirt right side out; press.

STEP 3. Baste ¼ inch from the top edge. Cut monofilament to the finished skirt width. Tie each end to a T pin, then lay the monofilament along the basting stitches. Zigzag-stitch over the monofilament ¼ inch from the skirt's top edge, pulling the monofilament to gather the skirt as you sew.

STEP 4. Cut a 4-inch-wide fabric band to match the finished skirt width plus 3 inches. With right sides together and raw edges aligned, center the band on the skirt top edge; sew together. Unfold; press open. Press band ends to the lining side of the skirt, even with the skirt edge. Press under ½ inch along the band's unsewn edge. Fold the band in half, enclosing the raw top edge; press. With the skirt right side up, sew through all layers ⅛ inch from the bottom edge of band.

STEP 5. Attach the adhesive-backed side of the fastening tape to the inside edge of the sink. Sew the remaining half of the fastening tape to the front of the skirt band. Hang the skirt, beginning at the center and working out.

# outdoor projects

## 294 Covert Cover-Up

### MATERIALS

- Two 8-foot pieces of 1x12 rough-cut cedar
- Six 2-inch butt hinges
- Four No. 8x1⅝-inch stainless-steel wood screws
- Paint or stain (optional)
- Table saw or circular saw
- Jigsaw
- Tape measure
- Speed square or clamp-on straightedge
- Drill with ⅛-inch, 1-inch Forstner, and ¼-inch Forstner drill bits
- Coffee can (36-ounce)
- Orbital sander and 120-grit sandpaper
- Clamps

### START TO FINISH

STEP 1. Use a speed square or a clamp-on straightedge as a guide for straight cuts. Cut ½ inch off both ends of each 1x12 cedar board to ensure straight edges. Cut two 40-inch-long pieces from each board.

STEP 2. Use the coffee can as a template to round one end of each 40-inch board. With the edge of the can flush with the top and left side of the board, mark a semicircle with a pencil. Move the can so it's flush with the right side of the board, and mark a second semicircle. The two semicircles should meet at the center top of the board, creating two arcs; see illustration, *right*. Cut ends with jigsaw.

STEP 3. If desired, draw or stencil a flower design 4 inches up from the bottom of the two end boards. Cut out designs with a jigsaw.

STEP 4. To form brackets, use leftover 1x12 pieces. Cut two 11⅛-inch square pieces. Save the scraps to make the shelves.

STEP 5. With speed square, draw a diagonal line from corner to corner on each square. Use lines as guides to cut pieces in half.

STEP 6. On each bracket, measure and mark each side 9 inches from the right angle. Using the coffee can as a template, draw a semicircle from each mark to the cut edge. Use a jigsaw to round the edges as shown *below*.

STEP 7. From the right angle of each bracket, measure 2 inches and then 2⅞ inches along one side. Mark each spot. From those marks, mark a 4½-inch notch into each bracket. The notch should be ⅞ inch wide, the same thickness as the wood. Cut out each notch with a jigsaw.

STEP 8. Cut a 4½-inch-long and ⅞-inch-wide notch in the center top (between semicircles) of each 40-inch-long board.

STEP 9. Mount brackets on the two end boards. On each of these brackets, measure 4 inches from the notch and 1 inch up from the bottom edge; mark. Remove brackets and drill a 1-inch hole with Forstner bit at marks on the two brackets.

STEP 10. Rip the scraps of cedar to 3 inches wide. Mount the brackets without 1-inch holes on the two center 40-inch boards. Hold a 3-inch shelf under each bracket. Mark each board where shelves should be mounted. Drill a ⅛-inch pilot hole at each mark. Use 1⅝ stainless-steel wood screws to attach shelf below bracket.

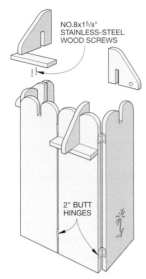

NO.8x1⅝" STAINLESS-STEEL WOOD SCREWS

2" BUTT HINGES

STEP 11. Remove brackets from boards. Arrange boards in the order they will appear. Lay first two adjacent boards next to each other, so inside edges are together. Clamp. Measure 4 inches from bottom of boards for location of bottom hinge. Measure 32 inches from bottom of boards for location of top hinge. Install hinges. Repeat this step for remaining two boards

STEP 12. To attach the two sets of boards together, set them in a W pattern and clamp the two inside boards together. Measure for hinge location as in Step 11. Install hinges (see *above*).

STEP 13. Sand, and paint or stain screen as desired. Install brackets.

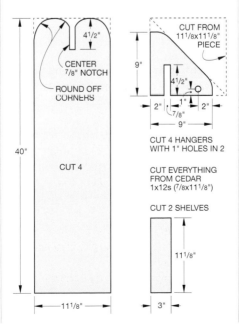

4½"

CENTER ⅞" NOTCH

ROUND OFF CORNERS

40"

CUT 4

11⅛"

CUT FROM 11⅛"x11⅛" PIECE

9"

4½"

2" ⅞" 1" 2"

9"

CUT 4 HANGERS WITH 1" HOLES IN 2

CUT EVERYTHING FROM CEDAR 1x12s (⅞x11⅛")

CUT 2 SHELVES

11⅛"

3"

## 295 Upward Bound

### MATERIALS

- One 8-foot-long pressure-treated 2x4
- Three 8-foot-long pressure-treated 1x4s
- One 8-foot-long pressure-treated 1x2
- Portable circular saw with a rip guide, or table saw
- 2-inch deck screws
- 1¼-inch deck screws
- ½-inch roofing nails
- 30 feet of 14-gauge solid, bare copper electrical wire
- Weatherproof glue
- Exterior-grade primer and paint
- Post-hole digger
- Crushed rock

### START TO FINISH

STEP 1. Follow the construction diagrams *right*. Paint all pieces before assembly.

STEP 2. Cut the decorative grooves into the face of each 1x4 post using a portable circular saw with a rip guide or a table saw.

STEP 3. Cut the upper and lower rails to length from 1x4 stock. Rip the upper rail 2½ inches wide. Rip and cross-cut the 1x2 upper cap, upper and lower filler, and trim to size.

STEP 4. Assemble the posts, rails, and caps with glue and screws, spacing them as shown. Drive all screws from the back, using 2-inch screws to hold the posts to the lower cap and 1¼-inch screws for all other assembly.

STEP 5. Place the trellis facedown on your work surface. Partially drive ½-inch roofing nails around the perimeter every 4 inches.

STEP 6. Secure one end of the copper wire to one of the nails in the upper rail by looping it twice around the nail. Then wrap the wire around itself. Take the wire to one of the nails in the lower cap. Loop it once or twice around each nail. Repeat, working in a gridlike fashion, using the diagram *below*. End the wire in the same way you began. Avoid excessive tension—pull only enough to keep the wire straight. String the horizontal wires in the same manner.

STEP 7. Dig holes for the trellis. Put crushed rock in the bottom for drainage. Hold the trellis plumb and backfill. Firmly tamp the soil with the end of a 2x4.

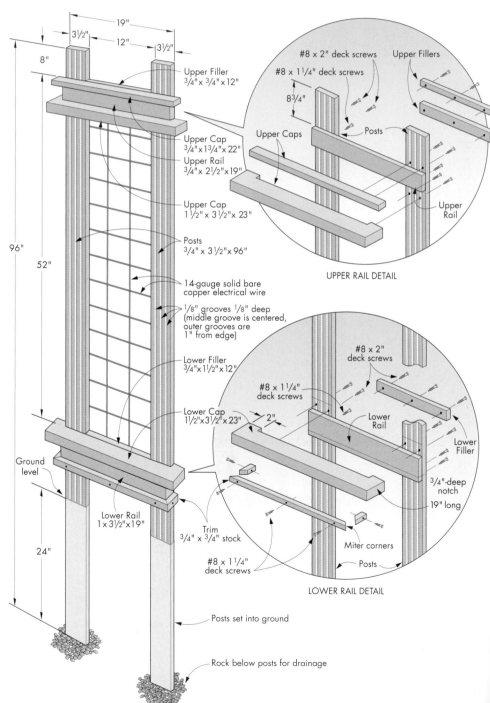

19"

3½" — 12" — 3½"

8"

Upper Filler
¾" x ¾" x 12"

Upper Cap
¾" x 1¾" x 22"

Upper Rail
¾" x 2½" x 19"

Upper Cap
1½" x 3½" x 23"

96"

52"

Posts
¾" x 3½" x 96"

14-gauge solid bare copper electrical wire

⅛" grooves ⅛" deep (middle groove is centered, outer grooves are 1" from edge)

Lower Filler
¾" x 1½" x 12"

Lower Cap
1½" x 3½" x 23"

Lower Rail
1 x 3½" x 19"

Ground level

2"

Trim
¾" x ¾" stock

24"

#8 x 1¼" deck screws

Posts set into ground

Rock below posts for drainage

#8 x 2" deck screws    Upper Fillers

#8 x 1¼" deck screws

8¾"

Upper Caps    Posts

Upper Rail

**UPPER RAIL DETAIL**

#8 x 2" deck screws

#8 x 1¼" deck screws

Lower Rail

Lower Filler

¾"-deep notch

19" long

Miter corners    Posts

**LOWER RAIL DETAIL**

# outdoor projects

## 296 Rock On

Order plans to make the rocker *above,* as well as the chair, footstool, and table on *page 221,* from Wood Plans, P.O. Box 349, Dept. DI-01, Kalona, IA 52247; 888/636-4478. Adirondack lawn chair #OFS-1001, $13.95; footstool and side table #OFS-1014, $10.95; rocker #OFS-1016, $13.95; all prices include postage. Visit http://woodstore.woodmall.com/index.html.

## 299 For the Birds

### MATERIALS
- One 10-inch cast-iron urn
- One 8-inch cast-iron urn
- Plastic-foam spheres (6- and 8-inch for urn toppers; 3- and 4-inch for smaller tabletop spheres)
- Two bags of birdseed (one each of black sunflower seeds and a birdseed mix)
- Creamy peanut butter
- Butter knife or frosting spatula
- Tree branch or chopstick
- Two rectangular pans or trays with sides, such as a jelly-roll pan or disposable plastic-foam tray
- Waxed paper

### START TO FINISH
STEP 1. Fill one of the pans with enough seed to evenly cover the bottom (*photo 1*). Set aside.
STEP 2. Place a plastic-foam sphere on a table covered with waxed paper. Using a butter knife or frosting spatula, spread peanut butter smoothly onto the sphere until it's completely covered (*photo 2*). To make the job easier, insert a chopstick or tree branch ½ inch into the sphere and use it as a handle to turn the sphere as you spread.
STEP 3. When the sphere is covered in peanut butter, roll it in the seed-filled pan. Use your hands to press birdseed firmly into place (*photo 3*). Continue rolling, as needed, until entire surface is covered.
STEP 4. Repeat for other spheres. Place completed spheres on another tray lined with waxed paper. Place in refrigerator for six to eight hours or until set.
STEP 5. Remove spheres from refrigerator; set larger ones on urns. Place the urns or the small spheres on an outdoor tabletop or in your garden. Beware: Birds love these creations so much that you'll need to refresh them with more peanut butter and seeds often.

## 300 Out of Sight!

### MATERIALS
- Eight 8-foot-long pressure-treated 2x4s
- Sixteen 8-foot-long pressure-treated 1x2s
- One 8-foot-long pressure-treated 2x10
- Circular saw and saber saw
- Drill with countersink bit
- 2-inch and 1¼-inch deck screws
- 13d galvanized nails
- Weatherproof glue
- Exterior-grade primer and paint
- Post-hole digger
- Crushed rock

### START TO FINISH
STEP 1. Follow the diagrams on *page 288* for construction details. Paint pieces before assembly.
STEP 2. Cut a 30-degree angle at the top end of each 2x4 post. Cut the 1x2 brackets; glue and nail each to the inner face of a post, centering it side-to-side and with the top end 1½ inches from the angled cut.
STEP 3. Create pointed tips for each of the 1x2 uprights with 45-degree cuts, then cut uprights to length. Cut 1x2 trellis rails, then nail the rails and uprights into a lattice assembly for each trellis.
STEP 4. Cut each 2x4 top rail to length; position it between posts and drive deck screws into

# outdoor projects

countersunk pilot holes from the back. Nail the lattice assemblies to the brackets.

STEP 5. Cut roof pieces and screw them into position. For the peaked top, join the two sides at a 30-degree angle. For the arched top, cut the post tops square as *right*. Glue together two 2x10s. Draw the radius using string and pencil.

STEP 6. Dig two 28-inch holes for each trellis. Place 4 inches of crushed rock in the bottom of each hole for drainage. Hold the trellis plumb while backfilling the hole. Firmly tamp the soil with a 2x4.

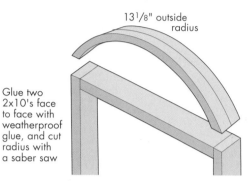

13¹/₈" outside radius

Glue two 2x10's face to face with weatherproof glue, and cut radius with a saber saw

ALTERNATE ROOF

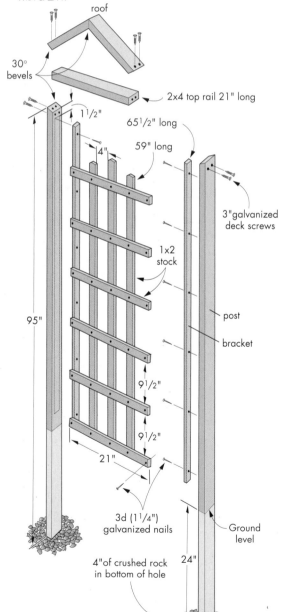

roof

30° bevels

2x4 top rail 21" long

1¹/₂"

65¹/₂" long

4"

59" long

3"galvanized deck screws

1x2 stock

95"

post

bracket

9¹/₂"

9¹/₂"

21"

3d (1¹/₄") galvanized nails

Ground level

4"of crushed rock in bottom of hole

24"

## mulching **matters**

Here are some tips for choosing the right mulch for your garden.

PINE NEEDLES (1). Pine needles form a mat, so they are less likely to blow away or shift. However, depending on your region, they may cost more than other mulches.

COCOA HULLS (2). Pricier than nuggets or shredded bark, cocoa hulls might be worth it for their chocolate aroma and fine texture.

WOOD SHAVINGS (3). Ask local cabinetmakers, carpenters, or builders to save wood shavings. They'll likely give them away for free or charge a small fee.

SHREDDED BARK (4). Cheap and easy to find, shredded bark is a popular choice. Cypress, eucalyptus, cedar, and other wood species are available at garden centers.

STRAW (5). Packaged in large bales, straw is widely available and modestly priced. It imparts a casual look to a garden.

BARK NUGGETS (6). Plentiful and inexpensive, bark nuggets are widely available at home and garden centers. However, they have a tendency to migrate into the surrounding lawn.

1

2

3

4

5

6